Incredible A...

THE COO

"D. Watkins's THE COOK UP is a bold, necessary dispatch from the streets, where a kid born into a hustler's life must fight for survival—and his soul. Watkins may have been a drug dealer, but he was caught up in his own addictions: to rampant consumerism, the numbness of Percocets, and a fantasy of the high-flying American dream. His book shows the astonishing evolution of a man who traded cheap fixes for the mighty power of the written word."

—Sarah Hepola, *New York Times* bestselling author of
Blackout: Remembering the Things I Drank to Forget

"Bleakly humorous, original prose, which pinballs between stoned, brand-focused, hip-hop excess and a more contemplative tone...Watkins provides a gritty, vivid first-person document of a desperate demographic." —*Kirkus Reviews*

"Accessible and edifying...In the tradition of James Baldwin's 'Letter from a Region in My Mind,' THE COOK UP is a personal history that complicates racial stereotypes...Watkins knows his readers live in different Americas. THE COOK UP is their invitation to notice one another standing in the same line."

—TheAtlantic.com

"Stunning." —*Baltimore City Paper*, Best Memoir 2016

"His compelling writing style has earned him a toehold among young black writers commanding national attention. Watkins' latest book, THE COOK UP: *A Crack Rock Memoir*, takes us deep inside Baltimore's drug trade and offers a rare glimpse into what it takes to escape that world." —WYPR.com

"D. Watkins is beautifully unusual. Having lived the horrors within the heart of our inner-city Baltimore firsthand and having acquired the heights of collegiate achievement, D. Watkins is uniquely equipped to communicate our political and social challenges of urban America not only through the lens of academia but through empirical knowledge as well. He is the voice of the future, seamlessly blending the wisdom of the streets and intellectual prowess in a way I have never experienced before."

—Jada Pinkett Smith

"The East Baltimore of D. Watkins is distant from where I live by twenty-five, maybe thirty blocks. It might as well be a country other than my own. This is the United States we abandoned and then forgot, the margins of a thriving, information-age America where mass labor is no longer essential, where the factories and warehouses and piers are empty or gone, and where Johns Hopkins University is the second largest employer—next to the illegal drug trade. And the corners are always hiring. That Watkins threaded his way from those corners to the page is rare enough. That he is so committed to pulling this world through with him—enough of it to at least rub our noses in it and make us acknowledge some collective responsibility—is precious. These are angry pages."

—David Simon, co-author of *The Corner* and creator of HBO's *The Wire*

"THE COOK UP delivers a raw and honest account of life in East Baltimore and a narrative of incredible strength and redemption. D. Watkins is truly an artist."   King Mez, hip-hop artist

"D. Watkins is his generation's David Simon. Another brilliant storyteller who takes you into the heart of East Baltimore and never flinches as he shows you the real."

—Touré, author of *Who's Afraid of Post-Blackness? What It Means to Be Black Now*

ALSO BY D. WATKINS

The Beast Side: Living (and Dying) While Black in America

THE
COOK UP

A CRACK ROCK MEMOIR

D. Watkins

GRAND CENTRAL
PUBLISHING

New York   Boston

Some names, relationships, and locations were changed to protect the innocent and the guilty.

Grand Central Publishing
Hachette Book Group
1290 Avenue of the Americas
New York, NY 10104

www.HachetteBookGroup.com

Printed in the United States of America

LSC-C

Originally published in hardcover and ebook by Grand Central Publishing.

First trade paperback edition: April 2017
10 9 8 7 6 5 4 3

Grand Central Publishing is a division of Hachette Book Group, Inc.
The Grand Central Publishing name and logo are trademarks of Hachette Book Group, Inc.

The Hachette Speakers Bureau provides a wide range of authors for speaking events. To find out more, go to www.hachettespeakersbureau.com or call (866) 376-6591.

The publisher is not responsible for websites (or their content) that are not owned by the publisher.

LCCN 2016440368
ISBN 978-1-4555-3726-6

To Devin AKA BIP, may you Rest in Power

INTRODUCTION

The War on Drugs is trash; it's just another way for the top 1 percent to benefit off of the pain that accompanies poverty. A bullet wound, a life sentence, or an OD for us is a paycheck for them, but there's hope—the new wave of white-suburban-Rice-Krispy-treat-after-school-soccer-program drug addicts may bring the change we all need.

I teach an English class at the University of Baltimore. We cover a range of topics dealing with culture and the way it's documented, and somehow drugs came up—"There's an awful heroin epidemic sweeping across our country," a small white woman with big eyeglass frames said, bursting into tears. "Our kids are quickly becoming addicted and dying!" She removed her frames to wipe her face before saying that she never thought her suburb would mirror a drug-infested city.

"Maybe it's new to you," I replied. "But if you're black and poor, the heroin epidemic has been around."

I showed them what East Baltimore was like in the 90's by telling them about Yellow Face Kerry with the short cornrows and how he liked to carry the same things to the park every day. A lighter, a tablespoon, a hypodermic needle, a belt that doubled as a tourniquet, and a sack of dope when he could swing it.

Kerry would strangle his calf with his belt till a few veins blushed and popped, then he'd flick, flick—flick the lighter until a sturdy flame hung under his tablespoon. His eyes flared as the fire made the spoon glow orange. The liquid contents inside bubbled until it reached the right temperature, one that he could only eyeball. Then he'd dab the tip of his needle into the heated solution until it filled the syringe. The next stop was in that rose-bruised calf vein where he sank the needle and pulled back the plunger until a little of his own blood flushed in, then a push returned that glob of dope-mixed blood back into his system as he loosened the belt and slipped into an easy nod.

He'd float away to wherever dope fiends float to, as the rest of us preteens would play basketball next to the bench he leaned on. Kerry didn't scare us, because his presence was normal—junkies, dope fiends, sales, shooters, base heads, or whatever your region calls them—were normal.

I've been a professional writer for two years now and away from the drug game for over a decade. It feels like eons since I parked European cars smack dab in the middle of poverty—jumped out like a pop star with pop star clothes on and received all of the praise from the other dealers, the ladies, the fiends, and basically everybody but the cops. Today I walk those same blocks as an advocate: a person who pulls kids away from the drug game, not by demonizing their actions but by exposing them to other options that kids like us don't normally get and by telling the truth about selling drugs—how the money doesn't match the risk and that it's a vicious trap that has captured them, me, and the dudes that came before. Again, this isn't new; it has been like that forever.

Back in the 70's, Nixon's War on Drugs planted the seeds, which were fertilized by Reagan and Bush in the 80's, then grew into the field of mass incarceration that was harvested and cosigned by Bill Clinton in the 90's. John Ehrlichman, Nixon's domestic policy chief, told Dan Baum of *Harper's Magazine* that Nixon's War on Drugs was meant to target black people.

"We knew we couldn't make it illegal to be either against the war or black, but by getting the public to associate blacks with heroin, and then criminalizing both heavily, we could disrupt those communities. We could arrest their leaders, raid their homes, break up their meetings, and vilify them night after night on the evening news," explained Ehrlichman. "Did we know we were lying about the drugs? Of course we did."

Their plan worked as we watched the number of African Americans being incarcerated soar past whites, to be released back into society as partial citizens. *Partial* because drug policies can easily make you unemployable, leave you ineligible for financial aid, public housing, and welfare. You are basically like a slave, a captured human with partial rights. What do you do for money? How do you assimilate? This is America, and everything costs something. Having nothing drives a person crazy, pushing them toward two realities—that of a user, or that of a dealer.

I use art to explain these things, and admittedly at times it's difficult. The drug game has changed. I'm a dinosaur, a house phone, a walking tombstone. Friends mentioned in the earlier version of *The Cook Up*, some of the guys that even made it to the book launch, are now dead and gone—RIP to Cheese and Pretty Boy Kory. There's a shortage of us thirty-somethings that barely crawled out of the 90's, leaving me to be one of the few cats from that era with positive insight. And trying to define those harsh times to these new dealers with their dyed dreads, painted-on jeans, and drug habits worse than the junkies they serve is tougher than a MIT algorithm. I don't understand their language, their moves, the selfies they take with their weapons, or the point of them *slangin*— the money is even less than when I was active.

But when the young bulls do listen I explain that in Baltimore, 97 percent of the people born into poverty die in poverty and I understand that *heroin dealer* is one of the few jobs that is always hiring. It's been like that in our inner cities and will continue to be like that until those unfair drug policies are changed. And the government and big business profit off of those same policies, so they aren't excited to change anything—which means it's up to us. We are responsible for getting guys like Yellow Face Kerry the help he needs and kicking the drugs out of our own communities.

What my student didn't know is that the current white addiction is not a new wave. Many articles have been published on the rampant drug use in white communities and how it surpasses use in African American communities, even though the media and stereotypes would lead you to believe the opposite. The wild card is held by these Percocet-slinging pharmaceutical companies who can't wait to have doctors prescribe the drug for anything from a slightly scratched pinky to a bad day—and I fully understand that addiction because the pills had me too; luckily the prescriptions weren't half as easy to get in the early 2000's as they are now.

So many people in white communities are going Percocet crazy that doctors are finally being called out for their role in creating the epidemic and forced to lessen the large amounts that they were shelling out, but it is too late. Percocets are like synthetic heroin so if the doctor cancels your prescription, you can get the same feeling from the street pharmacist and that's exactly what the white kids are doing. As a result, treatment centers are popping up everywhere—I hope this leads to us effectively addressing the issue of narcotics addiction.

I well up with depression when I think about Yellow Face Kerry and his battle with addiction. White people and those in more privileged areas are starting to feel the same; and even though I'd never wish that pain on anybody, I'm glad this problem is finally getting the attention it needs. I hope books like *The Cook Up* help raise the awareness we need to change these issues—but the first step is acknowledging that the War on Drugs is trash and that the top 1 percent gains from that pain.

D. Watkins
December 2016

When you learn, teach, when you get, give.
                    —*Maya Angelou*

My junior high school class, wish I stayed there
Illegal entrepreneur, I got my grades there
Blaming society, mad, it wasn't made fair
I would be Ivy League if America played fair

—*Nas*

THE
COOK UP

THE BEAST SIDE OF
BALTIMORE

I saw bullets rip through the faces of adolescents.

I saw mothers abandon their kids. I saw fathers go out for milk to never return. I saw kids turn into killers. Cops steal and grandparents raise infants around here.

I saw kids slap spit out of adults.

I saw the devil. I saw dude shake dude's hand before whipping out his gun and making dude put his hands up.

We go through midlife crises at fifteen around here.

I saw friends kill friends. I saw friends kill friends and then attend their wake. I saw teachers tell kids that they'd die like their parents or siblings. What does hope look like?

I saw shot dudes in wheelchairs be shot again while they sat in their wheelchairs.

I saw shots that made bodies flip. I saw colostomy bags burst, guts spill, brains on the curb, brains on the wall, brains by the car, contusions, limbs knocked off, faces rearranged, eyeballs, small intestines, and flesh chunks. I saw flesh sizzle like minute steaks.

We all self-medicate around here.

I saw murder after murder. I've smelled murder. I saw bodies rot. I read 150 teen obituaries—all with short bios. I know hate.

I saw barefoot families, I saw drug money buy churches, I saw hoop dreams spark and fade. I saw all types of dreams spark and fade. I saw house raids, I saw families evicted, I saw AIDS spread, I saw thousands made, and lost right in the middle of the place where cops enforce, terrorize and collect—I saw it.

I saw it all.

LOOKING FOR BIP

BANG! BANG! BANG!

Aunt Kim's front door almost thumped off the hinges, while I was rolling a celebratory blunt because College Park, Georgetown, Loyola, and a couple of other schools were letting me in.

"Kim, kill the music!" I said, looking through the peephole.

I opened the door without removing the latch to see Ron G prop both hands on his knees like kickstands, his oval belly peeking out of his shirt.

"Ron, what the fuck is up?" I said.

He breathed heavily. "Yo, find Gee. They shot Bip!" he said—with his pudgy face pinching through the door.

"What?" I opened the door to let him in, but he continued down the hall shouting.

"Gee! Gee! Where you at! We got a problem! Gee!"

I didn't believe that shit. My bro Bip's not dead. Did I hear shots? East Baltimore is a gun range, so I always heard shots. Shots ring out in east Baltimore all day—especially when it's hot out. People always get shot but not Bip. *Fuck Ron*, I thought.

"Kim, Ron lost his got damn mind!"

You'd have to be psycho to shoot at my bro. Bip was the neighborhood dope man, a real star. He employed everyone, paid cops, financed the lives of murderers, fed and housed ex-cons until they could feed and house themselves. Bip's like Superman mixed with Jesus. He's not dead.

Ron G's stupid—I think he dropped out of kindergarten. Plus he's on acid, sherm, loose pills, *and* some other shit—it probably wasn't even Bip, I thought.

I dialed Bip's cell to tell him how stupid Ron G was, but I only got the voice mail *"You reached the right nigga at the wrong time, hit me back—one."* *BEEP.*

"Kim, stay here and roll another blunt while I see what's up," I said.

She was all frowned up like "Be carefullllll!" Bip and I aren't her kids, but she always treated us like we were. I felt her anxiety in my chest as I bounced.

"Please, baby, be careful!" she called out again as I shut the door.

Bip was driving a T-Top Z300 that day. He bought it from a Jewish car wholesaler named Seth. Seth was known for getting cars with clean titles and untraceable paperwork for young dealers. Seth helped Bip get that 300, a GS, and my Acura. The front of our house was a car show.

Bip's 300 was whiter than untouched snow with an identical shade on the wheels. It had white piping and the inside was reupholstered with beet-juice-colored leather.

I saw it double-parked a block away from Kim's.

Everyone knew Bip's car—he called it blow. That day, it was right in front of the food spot CC's Carryout with the hazards on so I knew he was in the gathering crowd I saw. I couldn't wait to tell him the stupid shit that Ron had said, and, more important, how I got accepted into college. He's going to flip over the amount of schools I gained acceptance to, especially since none of the guys in our family ever went to college.

Bip was probably pushing up on a girl, I thought—we were on a mission to book and bone every woman that we weren't related to. Bip was winning—only because he's older. But I was on his heels and had gotten three phone numbers the previous day.

Hurk, my best friend and one of Bip's workers, spotted me swimming through the mob. Hurk towered over all of us like an NBA player—his knuckles practically scraped the ground when he walked.

"Dee, oh God, Deeee!" he cried.

Hurk ran up on me like a crazed fan. His long face balled like crumpled paper, his dreads whipped every which way as he came toward me. He squeezed me hard, like he was trying to make my shoulders touch.

"Shorty, Im'a murk dem niggas that rocked Bip, put that on my muther." Tears scaled his face. I remained silent but the crowd didn't.

Bip's not dead and Hurk's just looking for trouble; he's been like that since we were two. "Noooooooooooooo," he howled as I pulled away, "Get the fuck off me, Hurk, I need to catch my brova."

I just needed to get through the mob of gossipers. I thought he was probably stuck in CC's because there were a million people blocking the door. I elbowed through the crowd. Everyone gazed at me like I walked in class late. Wet eyes and bent faces circled the scene. I inched closer. The Koreans who ran CC's Carryout clutched their babies while peeking through the caged door.

A young black man, blood all over his face, covered by a still sheet laid stretched across the concrete. The dead kid had on orange-and-white CB34 sneakers freckled with blood poking out from under the sheet. Everybody in the hood had those kicks—I was wearing them—so that could have been anybody lying there. Someone moved the body and his arm dangled.

I saw Bip's diamond two-tone gold bracelet gleam.

I ducked under the yellow warning tape and pushed past the beat cop. The sheet folded down a little as I stood closer. Brains and blood everywhere. Then the noise stopped and a cold silence blanketed the crowd.

"Bip, get up!" I begged. "Get up. Come on!"

It was the first time he ever ignored me. "Please yo!"

The beat cop gathered himself and slammed me down next to my brother. He flipped me like a pissy mattress, positioning for a chokehold. Fuck fighting back. I wished I had died too.

MY BROTHER'S KEEPER

Did you ever idolize a person you could touch? Was him bragging that you were his little brother the biggest honor you could possibly imagine?

Did your big brother ever run a dope strip? A crack spot? Both?

At age eleven, you watched him run the courtyard from your cousin's second-story window, working for your uncle—serving customers, ducking cops, and bossing around dudes twice his age.

You knew he loved you because he took his earnings and bought you whatever you wanted; you didn't even have to ask.

You remember him counting all of that cash until his fingers cramped and then falling asleep with his Nikes on, and you would take them off, wipe them down, and then place them back into their original box because he was such a neat freak.

Selling drugs seemed legal where you lived and he taught you how to be extra careful because bodies dropped every day—big dudes, baby girls, OG's, fat aunts, city workers and all. Bullets ain't have no name and he taught you that. He taught you everything.

Then there was the day your brother realized that he didn't have to work for your uncle anymore. That he was smart enough to run his own shop and could triple his profits.

He sees you blending in with losers, being lazy and smoking weed all day. He realizes that you have no positive role models, not even him. He sees that you, his little brother, are failing in school and life.

He tells you these things bother him and that he's going to make a change. You know he's going to make a change because he's a doer. You want to be a doer too.

When you are twelve your big brother moves out—your feelings are split because you want to stay and leave with him. Your mom is a praying woman but she understands what it's like for you on these streets, and the rest of your family ignoring your exit makes your decision more than easy.

He puts you in a row home on Curley Street overlooking nothing and explains why he must hustle and why you must stay in school. You promise him that you will go to school and try hard. He gives you a stack of books to read about Frederick Douglass and Malcolm X because he came of age in an era when black awareness was at an all-time high. Rappers and dealers wore Afrocentric clothes, had a strong sense of negritude, and praised the motherland.

You didn't get it but you can't let him down so you try to understand; you read the books even though you hate reading. You scribble all in the margins in an effort to retain the information. It works a little. He's working too. His safe is full of cash, and so are your couch cushions and the Hefty bag in the closet.

You hear him and his crew living it up under the glowing streetlights every night. You want to live too. They post up and yell, "Blue tops of Cosby nose, blue tops of Cosby nose!" They trade Big, Pac, Nas, and Jay Z lines, fussing over who is the best. Others slap box, and pretty girls come past to chill, all on the same block that is flooded with laughing drug addicts who dance to songs only they can hear, and the fun never ever stops.

You see it all in a thousand-mile-per-hour blur—their jokes, their smiles, their corner—where transactions are made before the police hop out with cocked pistols, causing everyone to scatter. Sometimes they make arrests; sometimes they just beat on black teens with gun handles and wooden batons until they spit out blood, lunch, and teeth.

Gentrification peeked in but ran in fear. You don't run. You can't because your older brother wouldn't run. He taught you that heroes are afraid to run.

Years pass and your big bro, your idol, is still the king of east Baltimore, the reigning champ of the block. You realize that he's what you want to be. You even try to step outside to greet his crew and join in the drug talk. "Y'all rockin off a lot of coke out here!" you say, looking for approval. He laughs at you and says, "You finish those books? I got more!"

You reply, "Fredrick Douglass says, 'If there is no struggle, there is no progress' and 'Once you learn to read, you will be forever free.'"

He smiles and spits three more Douglass quotes, six more facts about things you and the other guys on the corner have never heard of and then another twelve book titles that you need to read.

You could never stump your brother. He didn't go to school but he was smarter than every teacher you ever had. He sends you back in the house with your head down. You know the corner isn't for you and he has no trouble reminding you.

You really don't know what's for you because you're his shadow.

People see you and speak of him. He wants you to be a reader and not a hustler. You don't want to read, you want to hustle, but you still do what he says.

You're fifteen now. That original crew he slang with under the lights are all dead and have been for a while. He has a whole new staff with similar looks and names. You see three or four new sets of new people every year. There's a low employee retention rate in his business.

You used to weep at funerals: every death used to feel new. Death started feeling the same. You used to wear suits to funerals but they've become so common now that you just show up in jeans and a hoodie, if you show up at all. Your brother is beyond successful. He's still out front, but also up the street now and around the corner too. He celebrates by giving you cash and buying nice cars.

You love your brother's gold ropes. They scream wealth. You always try his on when nobody's around. They give you power and connect the two of you. They make you handsome and interesting. Without them you are frail. You look in the mirror and see that your face is chubby and naked; you both share the same blank stare but you wonder when your face will tighten like his, when will your lip carry the same mustache. Adding the ropes makes you forget about the physical imperfections you see. They make you taller, smarter, more mature and polished. They make you complete.

He buys you some little chains as a reward for doing well in school. You wear them proudly, never tucking them in.

Seventeen and you are finally, almost, as popular as him. You have studied him religiously. You own his walk, his talk, his laugh. You drive his cars even though he bought you your own.

You now get his vision for your life and don't care about selling drugs or being a thug anymore. You like school and even apply to some colleges. Mr. Brown, your high school history teacher, recognized your potential and set you up with some SAT prep courses so that your test scores can be as high as your GPA. You study the courses, take the test, do well and start visiting colleges. Your brother goes with you to visit the University of Maryland's campus. You catch your tour guide checking his jewelry; he notices too and you both laugh.

A few more visits go down and some of those colleges let you in. The ones you'd least expect. You celebrate with your aunt because your big brother isn't around. She yells, "My baby got into Georgetown!"

You reply, "I'd be in Harvard if America wasn't so racist!"

You both laugh, crack jokes, and blast music. She doesn't know the difference between Georgetown and Harvard, she was just proud. You never saw a person look as proud as she does on that day—that makes you proud. You may never see that look again. Heaven came to that apartment and stayed until Ron G beat on the door.

You dress up for this funeral. Death feels new again.

You see wall-to-wall people there. They all look foreign. They never came around when he was alive. They all reach out but you don't reach back. Your eyes look puffy, the lower lids inflamed. They look like you are in the eleventh round of a twelve-round fight. You're losing. You can't fight any longer.

Burying him in his jewelry is the only thing that makes you happy. He always told you about Egyptian kings being buried with their favorite items, food they loved, and their best jewelry. You want to be buried with your favorite things too; you want to be buried with him.

Weeks pass and you are still paralyzed by his death. You can't leave your crib. You consider moving to a new crib to escape the pain, hoping it won't feel the same. There's only one way to make this type of pain stop. He used to keep a pearl .357 Magnum under his bed; it was smooth and deadly, just like him. You keep it under your bed now.

You reach for it. It's fully loaded. You empty the bullets onto your mattress and then pick one up and look at it—it's not too heavy, but heavy enough to erase your pain. You drop it in the chamber.

Spin spin spin ...

The cold steel is connected to your temple with no space in between. You close your eyes and rub the trigger. It feels right. You squeeze. *Click!* You squeeze again and hear another click, a louder click. It's the loudest click you ever heard, louder than bombs dropping on crowded towns. Nothing happens. Night darkens the room. You doze off next to the gun, praying that you don't wake up.

AFTERMATH

Two weeks after Bip died on the concrete, one week after his funeral where a collage of ex-girlfriends, junkies, and gangstas packed every corner of a Baptist church we never attended—all screaming louder than newborn crack-babies—I sat.

Alone in the same corner of my house, in the same clothes, looking at the same Polaroids wondering who would do this. Who? Who could kill my bro and why?

My mom called me every day, telling me to pray. Bip wasn't her son but she felt his loss through me. I got on my knees and looked up at God for an answer two or three times a day but never got a response.

A lot of us have to put all of our faith in heaven because our lives here on earth are so messed up—the afterlife has to be better than the pain that comes with black skin.

East Baltimore is a place where people come and go. Loyalty, not blood, makes you family here because people are gained, trusted, and loved as quick as they fade. Some began to resurface after Bip passed. I felt like half of the city had stopped past my crib. They all had wild theories on what happened. A regular shooting transforms into a global massacre by the time it reaches the fifth dude. I wasn't really trying to hear it. Some really wanted to offer condolences but most came because they heard I was giving away

13

Bip's old things. I passed out bags of hoodies, leather coats, and unworn sneakers.

A steel battering ram ripped our door from its frame two days after his murder. Narcs buried my face in carpet while they tossed around my belongings. A bacon-colored captain stood over me. "The murder was drug related, son, this is normal procedure!" His coworkers looted our home, leaving only the items with no value. I managed to hold on to some jewelry but the bulk of our goods were placed on drug hold, or so they say.

The cops were so busy taking jewelry, and Sony products, they didn't even notice the two-hundred-pound safe in the basement. Bip used to tuck money and gems in there, and he taught me how to open it in case of an emergency. But I couldn't care less about that safe or any material thing in general. Bip—my influence, my definition of family, the person who made me inquisitive, the one who taught me everything from how to play basketball, how to save money, and how to study to how to drive, and how to protect my face in a fight—was a memory.

SHOOTERS

My homie Nick came through with weed to smoke every day. Nick is chubby with chubby features and covered in faded basement tattoos. He lives in a Yankees cap and all of his white tees touch his knees. He's the first kid I met way back when we moved down to Curley Street.

I whipped him in a game of one-on-one over at Ellwood Park when we were twelve and he said, "You can beat me in basketball, but I bet you can't beat me fighting!" We fought, both claimed victory, laughed it off, and have been tight ever since.

Weeks after Bip died, Nick would ask me about college and I'd just ignore him. I had thought about all of the schools I'd gotten into but I didn't care about any of it. I had to shake Bip's murder.

Every night, I'd hear Bip scream, "Deeeeeeeeeee, where's my phone!" I'd pop up, and then check every room, flipping sofa cushions and rambling through desk drawers like a maniac until I realized that Bip was not there and he wasn't coming back. Then I'd bolt downstairs, peek into the alleyway, unlock and relock every door and window before checking on his .357 under my couch, and making sure my .45 under my pillow was loaded.

Bip taught me how to shoot when I was thirteen. Nick tagged along too. We'd line cans up inside of the empty pavilion in the

15

middle of Ellwood Park after hours and buck shots at them one by one.

"I'm only teaching you how to shoot for protection. Remember, any coward can use a gun," said Bip, mangling logos dead in the center of every can. Nick tried to hold the gun sideways like the guys in hood movies. He eyed a Sprite can while extending the pistol—*POP!* The bang slung Nick to the ground with the gun flying in the opposite direction. He received more damage than the can he was aiming at.

"I'm good, Yo!" screamed Nick, popping up, rubbing his arms, pulling his dick and making sure that the rest of his body parts were still attached.

"That's a lesson!" Bip laughed. "Never hold a gun like a dumb nigga in a hood movie! This ain't Hollywood, this Holly-hood! Dee, you up next!"

I picked up the gun that embarrassed Nick and squeezed the handle with both hands, tight enough to feel my veins pop. It warmed my skin as remnants of smoke from Nick's attempt swam past my target. The soda can was perfectly aligned with my front sight. I looked at Bip; he looked at the can and then gave me a nod.

I delivered two shots, the first hitting the can, the second hitting where the can once stood. "Lemme try again, Yo!" Nick yelled, still massaging his arm. I passed him the pistol.

"Good job, boy! But remember, anyone can shoot a gun, real niggas use these," Bip said, holding up his fists like trophies.

I wish that statement was true, but I was smart enough to know that it didn't matter if you were considered to be "real" or "fake"—people didn't fight with their hands anymore.

COPING TACTICS

Ay Yo, Biggie my favorite rapper but he say some gay-ass shit like, *'Girl, you look so good huh, I'll suck on ya daddy dick'* and I'm like, 'Yo! What type of homo shit is that?'" yelled Nick from downstairs.

"Word, that line is mad suspect," I replied, digging in my ashtray, looking for a blunt butt to spark.

"I'm a call this weed and roll some pussy. I mean... You know what I mean, nigga. You want some weed and some pussy, right?" Nick said, flopping on the couch ass first.

"Yo, Dee, Biggie a handsome fat nigga like me. That's why I fuck with him. He made fat niggas sexy, though, you feel me?"

I laughed as I went back upstairs and climbed back into my bed, wondering what it would be like not to feel. Emotions are unneeded baggage that won't allow me to be anything but a broken person who weeps in isolation. If I was as smart as I thought I was, I'd be able to teach myself not to feel. My sheets smelled like bud and underarms. Bip's RIP balloons were past deflated and sagging over my dresser.

"I'ma bring the blunt up to you, bro!" hollered Nick.

Nick tried his best to help me cope with losing Bip. His idea of coping meant good weed, lots of Belvedere, and being an ear even though I didn't say much. He tried to make me laugh every day and sometimes it even worked. More importantly, Nick helped me move all of the books, sneakers, and everything else that belonged to Bip out of the house. Dump the clothes, dump the memories, dump the pain, or so I thought. Some of those memories remained undumpable: Bip's bookstands, Bip's push-up bars, the matching recliners we sunk into when watching playoff games, his spare car keys on my dresser.

His smell—Polo Blue—lurked around corners, his toothbrush, hairbrush, and flat razors. "Fuck is my razors at, D!" he'd yell on date nights. Bip's half-eaten crab cake was still in the fridge, his boxes of Raisin Bran, Mistic Pink Lemonade iced tea—his official drink—his posters, his toiletries, and his pictures.

I had to get off of Curley Street.

Milton, the same guy who rented us the place on Curley, had a corner house in back of a alley for me on North Castle Street—about two miles north. The boarded-up homes that filled the neighborhood made it look like a crackhead resort.

He wanted six hundred dollars a month, which was cool. I thought I could look for a job while I lived off of the eight thousand and some odd dollars that I had saved up from Bip's allowances. College could wait.

Nick needed a place too, so I told him that he could move in for three hundred dollars a month and we could split the utilities along with the cable bill straight down the middle. He was cool with that, so I signed the lease and paid the first three months in cash.

Nick sold a little weed too, when he could get it. It wasn't the best or the worst—mid-grade with small traces of orange hair and every once in a while you found a seed. He was no Scarface but he raked in enough dough to cover his share of the bills, and if he couldn't, we could always get money from Hurk.

Hurk and I met in the towers. His mom sucked dick for crack until she became too hideous to touch. By the time I was thirteen, her gums were bare, her skin peeled like dried glue, chap lived on her lips and she always smelled like trash-juice. Her last days were spent panhandling on Fayette Street and getting a puff or two off of old cigarette butts she found smashed in the pavement. Eventually AIDS took her out of her misery.

Hurk's my age. When we were kids, his family was about a billion dollars below the poverty line. All of his jeans had shit stains because he didn't have underwear or running water, and he had so many holes in his shoes that his feet were bruised. Shortly after we met, I started giving him clothes that I didn't want and he stayed with us most nights. We became brothers.

At thirteen, Hurk started hustling for Bip and never looked back. He loved his job. Hurk was organized, and he worked harder than anyone else on the corner. Like a little Bip, Hurk beat the sun to work every morning—four a.m. in the blistering cold, with bright eyes and fists full of loose vials.

He never messed up the count and seized every advancement opportunity. His workload tripled after Bip passed, but he called every day and came by when Nick and I moved into the new place.

"Dee, how you holdin' up, shorty?" said Hurk.

"I don't even know. Man, I been in the bed for weeks," I replied.

"Naw, nigga, get out. Get a cut, nigga, go do some shit! Least you still alive!"

"You right," I said as I sat on the edge of my bed.

"What the fuck, Yo, you cry every day?" Hurk asked.

"Naw, well no, shit, I dunno."

"Yo, anyway I'm gonna murder dat nigga that popped Bip. Ricky Black bitch ass. You go live, nigga, get some new clothes, pussy or sumthin'."

I picked up my head for the first time in days. "I didn't even know my bro had static with him."

The drama that comes with murder made Hurk excited. He leaped from his seat.

"I don't know why he killed Bip. But they saying it's him, he was always a hata. But whatever, Yo, I'ma get dat nigga!"

I told him he was crazy, but I didn't care. I wasn't happy or sad, just indifferent and used to murder. I wouldn't commit that murder—I'm not a killer. I am capable of hate. I hate Ricky or whoever did this, and I am a direct product of this culture of retaliation. A culture that did not allow me to sleep, eat, or rest until I know that Bip's killer is dead. It didn't even matter if Hurk or I killed Ricky or not because someone would eventually. Bip received love from almost every thug in the city, so someone would avenge his death.

"I gotta go, I got dope to sell, brova. I love you!" said Hurk, fixing his jeans, preparing to exit.

"Be careful," I said.

"Nigga, I keep the ratchet on me," he replied while lifting his sweatshirt to show me the gun planted on his waist. He also said that he had an HK in his backpack with a bunch of rounds that clicked against each other when he moved.

"Better to get caught with a hammer than without it, ya dig?" I said while showing him to the door.

"You should think about school, D. Bip would like that. Plus I won't be around too much, Yo, I'm on the run for some bullshit. They sayin' I shot somebody. Da cops kicked my girl's crib in at four a.m. and everything!"

"Damn, you did it?"

"Who knows, but fuck the police, I'll holler!" said Hurk, flapping on his hood and walking out.

A DIFFERENT WORLD

Going away to school would have been too much for me three months after Bip's death. Campus housing, adjusting to life in another city, and late registration all while wearing my depression like an overcoat was a reality I couldn't handle, so I decided to attend Loyola, a local school on the edge of Baltimore.

I always thought college would be like that show *A Different World*. Dimed-out Lisa Bonets and Jasmine Guys hanging by my dorm—young, pure, and making a difference. I'd be in Jordans and Jordan jerseys or Cosby sweaters like Ron and Dwayne Wayne, getting A's and living. No row homes, hood-rats, housing police, or gunshots—just pizza, good girls, and opportunity.

Loyola was a GAP commercial—miles and miles of grass, new construction, and healthy smiles. I saw kickball and flag football and people holding hands. A universe of white and Asian faces smirked at me as I walked across campus the first day. This was a different world, but not the one I was looking for.

There were some other black guys there, but they weren't black like me. They spoke proper English, called each other dude, wore pastel colored sweaters, Dockers, and boat shoes, carried credit cards, chased Ugg-booted-white girls, played sports other than basketball and talked about Degrassi—*What the fuck is Degrassi?*

I wore six braids like Iverson, real Gucci sweat suits like my brother, and about a fifteen-thousand-dollar mixture of my and Bip's old jewelry. It was my first experience interacting with other races, and that, combined with my Rasta weed habit, made me paranoid so I talked Nick—who had dropped out of middle school long ago—into hanging around campus with me.

"Yo, Dee, if any of these people act dumb, even the da principal, tell me. Swear to God I'll fuck 'em up for you, Yo."

"Colleges have deans, Nick, not principals, but I guarantee I won't have any problems here."

Each day, I'd float through Loyola clean and high. Some of the students were racist—but not to my face, and it probably wasn't their fault, most of their parents gave them racism as a first gift. A few of my professors looked at me as if I was speaking a different language when I answered questions. My philosophy teacher, a tweed coat–wearing dickhead was the worst; every class he'd say, "What sport did you play to get into here?" I honestly thought about having Nick pistol-whip him, but he was only a pedestrian on my road to bigger goals.

I started meeting people and even tried to adjust to the campus culture by attending basketball games and buying a gray Loyola hoodie. I bought Nick a black one. Together we'd sit through home games, underwhelmed by the basic style of play and unaffected by the school spirit that shook the gym. Loyola students get excited over made free throws and baseline jump shots. Hood dudes like us need to see thrills: dunks, spin moves, shit talking, finger pointing, and ankle-breaking crossovers.

Eventually, I met some cool white boys to smoke weed with. Tyler was a freshman like me but already had a hold on the campus. Girls giggled when he spoke, and most of the other freshmen lived and died for his approval. I saw him around a few times but initially we met in the Athletic Center. I was shooting jumpers and Nick was rebounding for me. Tyler walked up and said, "Nice shot. You guys gamble?"

"Shoot his head off, Dee! Shoot his head off, Dee!" chanted Nick. Tyler and I went five dollars a shot for an hour or so and I think he beat me out of two or three hundred dollars. I paid him and he gave me a hundred back.

"What's this for?" I said, rejecting the money. He explained that he had gambled with black guys before and he noticed that the winners always give the losers a little something back. Then he said: "Besides, you guys smell like Jamaicans! Can I get some of that?" The three of us walked back to Nick's Camry and smoked some joints. Tyler thought the bud was decent; Nick and I always had it so we exchanged numbers.

Sometimes we smoked and talked trash to girls together, or beat the shit out of the squares that hung around in the gym in basketball. Tyler even took me to his spot in Bolton Hill, a neighborhood filled beautiful brownstones that ran from $300K to almost a million.

Tyler liked Jay Z, 2Pac, and watched *Above the Rim*, just like me. I turned him on to chicken cheese steaks with hots from Mama Mia's. He exposed me to the richer parts of city like Mount Vernon and Guilford, where there wasn't a black person in sight—places I didn't even know existed.

I understood all of his white boy slang like *puke* or *dude* or *riffle*, which means to steal. White boy slang is easy. But I had to explain some language to him that he couldn't pick up in context—like *unk* meaning uncle, everybody's name is Yo or dummy, and how we say *dug* instead of *dawg* or dog and Vick. White people liked to buy eighths of weed but black people buy Vicks. A Vick is seven grams and we call them Vicks because Michael Vick wore number seven.

I really liked Tyler but most of his friends were hard to take. They'd invite me and Nick to campus parties. We'd walk in and the mood would change. They'd reference Dr. King and then Dr. Dre, and call us bro and brotha, and give us too many handshakes. They tried to imitate us so we felt more comfortable, but it just felt condescending. Luckily, we never got into any fights and the N-word never slipped out. The parties got old to us really quick so we stopped going.

My mother being super proud was the best part. She'd tell all of her church friends that I was doing well in School and hit me on the jack like "College man, you need anything?" I'd always say no, and pretended like everything was ok. An artificial front that I started believing myself.

I faked like doing homework and adjusting to this new world helped me deal with the loss of Bip, but in reality I still had sleepless nights where I sat in the park until the sun came up, wondering why I was alive, why Hurk had such a short temper, why couldn't Nick study and be a student too, and why I didn't get a chance to tell my bro what he meant to me. By mid-semester I was sick of school. The work wasn't hard, but it was boring as that show *MASH*. I feel like anybody can listen to a teacher, read a book, and then solve a problem. And trying to assimilate was even more exhausting.

What would my brother say if he saw me hanging around the cafeteria with Zack Morris and Carlton Banks, laughing at jokes I hated, listening to stories that bored me, going to wack basketball games, slowly conforming—being a good Negro. What would he say if he caught me referencing *Degrassi*? Bip didn't want me in the streets, but I know he didn't want this—we were raised by Biggie, Spike Lee, Pac, NWA, and Public Enemy, not this Wayne Brady shit.

So I said fuck it.

THAT RED SAFE

That first semester at Loyola, I was down to about $2,900, sharing a car with Nick, and had no income. Pain stared back when I glanced in the mirror and basically my whole demeanor looked manic-depressed.

I was sick of school and knew it was time to crack Bip's safe. I could ease some pain with the cash and look for a job while I figured this life shit out. The key for me was not to blow all the money on stupid things like cars, clothes, and fun—really the only stuff eighteen-year-olds cared about.

The safe was red and rusted. It had to weigh about two hundred pounds. I remember when Bip bought it from a pawn shop on Monument Street. The guy wanted five hundred dollars but he talked him down like, "Man, you know what I spent up in here? Hook a brotha up and knock a little off. You want me to have a lil something to put in there, right?"

Those guys at the shop discounted it because they loved Bip. Then they spent about fifteen minutes explaining the functions and talking about how it was fireproof and could probably survive a nuke. It took two fiends to lift it, which says a lot because crack gave junkies superhuman strength.

I had a junkie I was cool with named Bucket and he, along with one of his friends, carried the safe up to my room and tucked it into the closet.

I looked at it every day. I knew there was something valuable inside. I just had to make sure I was ready for it.

MY TRUST FUND

Nick and I along with three girls from around the way sat in my room over a fifth of Grey Goose, warm pizza, and some well twisted blunts. They all laughed, I just thought about the safe. *What's in it? What if it's empty? I know he wouldn't leave it empty. What should I do with the money?* Nick was cool when drunk, and we had been drinking seriously for a while, but the girls were annoying. The kind of annoying that's not cute—young, loud, and annoying. I didn't know them and really wasn't trying to meet them. My focus was on the safe.

"Hey, ladies, no disrespect but y'all gotta go," I said, moving everyone out into the hallway.

"What the fuck!" they replied from the other side of the door. I opened it and put the Goose and pizza on their side. Our place was a real teenager bachelor pad with no decorations, blank walls, Nike boxes stacked, and nothing in the fridge but Fruit Roll-Ups. Nick had a collection of empty Hennessy bottles on the counter-top. All of our dishes were paper and all of our cups were plastic and red. We really had nothing but a bunch of sneakers, some air mattresses, and that safe.

I locked my door and kneeled in front of the safe. The numbers were a little faded, but clear enough for me to make them out: 02-right-10-right-08-left-19-right-02.

Bip taught me how to open it blindfolded so that I could crack it under any circumstance. I remember when we used to have to lie on our backs and kick the door closed because he had so much money in there.

I had to give the handle an extra tug because it was a little rusted around the edges. I dropped my weight and the door flung open. All types of shit spilled out. I slowly started pulling out the contents and laying them on the floor around me. Stacks and bundles of balled up and unseparated cash, receipts, a watch, maybe a brick and a half of Aryan-colored cocaine, about half a brick of heroin, two pistols, a big zip of vials, a Michael Jordan rookie card in a plastic case, and some pictures: mostly Polaroids of naked girls from our block, a few party pics, and then one of us. Me as a toothless kid with dreads at the top of my fade wearing a red 76ers Starter jacket propped up on Bip's bony shoulders. He was wearing the same jacket and haircut. No facial hair, no worries, no problems. Just us and our U-shaped smiles. The back of it read "Bip and Lil Dee Dunbar v. Mervo 91."

Nick knocked on my door.

"Yo, Rita wanna fuck you, nigga, stop buggin'. Come on out!" he yelled.

Juvenile's "Ha" remix was cranking, making our thin walls shiver. I guessed they had continued the party downstairs. I cracked the door.

"Nick, cut that shit off and put them out. I need to show you something." My cold stare sparked urgency in him.

I slammed the door in his face and started reloading the safe. I put the coke and about three double handfuls of cash back in. I also threw the receipts and pistols in as well. I tacked the picture of us up over my bed and locked the safe just in time to hear Nick say, "Dee, we good? Lemme in."

"Yeah, Nick, come in, the door's open."

Nick walked in with his .45 drawn and cocked. "Wassup, dug?"

He looked over and saw the pile of cash. "Niggas is rich" came out of his mouth over and over again. Nick had never seen that amount of money stacked up like that—but I had.

I knew we weren't rich and I could easily eyeball a pile of street money. My guess was about $70K minus what I stuffed back into the safe. In Nick's defense, $70K in street money could easily look like two million dollars to the naked eye. Street money is thick, wrinkled, tatted, bulky, and fluffy—every dollar has a story.

I told Nick that we had a decision to make. I still had mixed feelings about selling drugs. I never set out to be a part of that life, but that never stopped that life from setting out to be a part of me. Eighteen, with more than a hundred thousand dollars in cash and product—I could probably open a business. Or I could give the drugs away and start with a clean slate, maybe even go back to school—a real black college like in *A Different World*.

But I knew I didn't want school and I didn't know anything about a legal business, so why not? Every neighborhood I lived in was flooded with fiends—burned-out people who all wanted the same thing, an escape, which is what I had. Nobody else gives a fuck about this drug shit, so why should I? Why should I care?

Junkies are killing themselves, I thought to myself over and over again. This shit is bigger than me, bigger than everything.

"So look, Nick, this coke looks really, really, *reallyyy* good. It's probably better than ninety-nine percent of the shit on this planet. You gonna help me move it and we gonna split the money fifty-fifty. I'm thinkin' we should break it up into ounces and go dirt cheap like $550 to $650 to the niggas we like and seven hundred a joint to everyone else, because it's all profit."

"Hell NO! Did you try some of that shit?" he replied.

Nick said that we would be leaving a ridiculous amount of money on the table. I said, "I know but I don't want to get stuck with it, and I'm not slanging hand-to-hand on anybody's block." Nick said that he would do all of the dirty work and I wouldn't have to touch a thing, not a single vial. "Naw, I'll earn my share," I said.

Nick was right. That coke looked too good to be wholesaling ounces; asking for $650 would be like giving it away. I figured that I was already taking the risk of getting a kingpin charge with all of this coke lying around so I might as well maximize my profit margin. I told Nick I'd assemble a crew and that we could cap up half of the coke into $10's, $20's and $30's, put it over in Bucktown by Ellwood Park and let it sell itself. "And wholesale the other half for $950 a joint?" he said.

"Naw, Nick, I'ma cook that into crack. Watch me fry."

Nick nodded in agreement as he tucked his pistol in his waistband. Nick has a five-year minimum sentence strapped to his hip, I thought, as I looked at the pile of twenty-five to life in front of us on the floor. I had another hundred-plus years inside of the safe with another twenty years stashed under my bed.

HOPE

Hope was like my big sister. She always called me li'l bro even though she knew I had a stupid crush on her back in the day. Hope lived over in Bucktown, right across the street from where Nick and I planned on dumping product. I hadn't kicked with her for some time but I was happy that I had reason to chill in her neighborhood. We could catch up and smoke while we clowned around about old shit.

Hope was about four years older and born supermodel ready with high-ass cheekbones, Colgate ad teeth, and dark, curly hair that reached her hips when braided. She looked a little better than a young Vanessa Williams.

Hope is from my old building but you wouldn't know it. Her mom kept her far away from the street dudes and riffraff. She was active in the arts, never hung around public housing, and spoke perfect English, which is why I was startled when I found out she was dating Brock—a two-bit hustler from west Baltimore.

We used to call him Ugly-Yo and he'd proudly answer. Brock looked like a brown Shrek with thinning dreadlocks. His personality was as ugly as his face.

Hope and Brock shared a second-floor apartment and I had been through there once or twice. She knew how to create those impossible Ikea-looking store displays with glass ball–filled vases on modern tables over multicolored rugs. She also had pieces of her own artwork on the wall, mostly abstract stuff with deep meanings I didn't get. The combination of her spirit and creativity made the place glow, despite it being in the center of a fucked-up neighborhood—think of a diamond surrounded by a bunch trash.

A few days after I cracked the safe, I decided to hit her up.

"Hey, Dee, baby!"

"What's up Hope? How you been?"

"Not so great, can we talk? In person?"

I told her to say no more. I figured that Brock dumbass probably did some something stupid.

I pulled up to a murder scene. A kid had got his melon cracked a few steps away from her house. Police and homicide squads give me anxiety so I wrapped a blunt and tucked it. I hoped Hope still smoked.

The mob around the murder stretched way past her door. In these scenes, there's always a grandma crying and a dude in a tank top spazzing out like "Yo, I'm kill dem niggas! All of Dem! I swear ta GOD!" all in front of the cops. That dude is normally bluffing—he's not going to kill anything. He probably works a nine to five and runs a Bible study. The crazy act looks good, but it's just a show. Real killers don't say a word, they just catch you and blow your head off.

I got a little a peek at the body but I didn't know who it was so I maneuvered closer and made my way to Hope's steps. She had been watching the scene from the door and waiting for me. She greeted me with a soft kiss on the cheek and we rolled up to her unit.

Shockingly her place was dirty and smelled worse than the dead guy out front. There were piles of cruddy dishes everywhere, empty pizza boxes on top of empty chicken boxes falling from the trash can, crawling with roaches, and collections of Hefty bags with weird clothes all over the place—I kinda didn't want to sit on the couch. I was scared that the odor of her apartment would get into my sweats.

"Damn, Hope. You good?" She glanced away and twiddled her thumbs. She looked dirty as well. She wasn't raised like that. I wondered if she was a junkie. I didn't really know how to ask in a polite way so I just came out and said, "Hope! You a junkie?"

She batted her big eyes. "No, silly, I'm just going through some shit." Junkie or not, she was still beautiful. Her cheekbones were regal.

"Dee baby, you think you could loan me some money until I get back on my feet? I would never ask you for anything. I don't know what to do."

She had to be getting high or desperate to ask me.

"Damn, Hope. I don't know what I'm holdin', how much do you need?"

She said a thousand dollars. I told her that I'd let her know a little later. I told her I wanted to make sure that Nick and I were in good shape.

But I really wanted to make sure she wasn't a fiend.

"What, you outta work?" I asked.

"Yeah, Brock kept calling my job and they fired me. I'm going to find something else but I'm pregnant."

"Pregnant!"

Yuck was my first thought but I didn't say anything. I'd give her a couple dollars; it wouldn't kill me but would be everything to her.

COOK UP

Nick, can you run me over to Hope's spot—she needs me," I asked while separating some cash into three even stacks of a thousand each.

"You fuckin' her raggedly ass? Let's get waffles first. I'm fuckin' barkin'!"

"Naw, she cool, and we'll eat later." I rubber-banded the cash and we hopped in Nick's Camry.

A few weeks had gone by since I cracked the safe and I didn't try to sell a single vial. I spent the time planning, scouting locations, and building a crew—stuff that corporations do. I also hired Hurk a lawyer. He did some research and recommended that Hurk turn himself in. The lawyer said the state's case was as soft as baby shit because the informant was sketchy and not coming to court. He had guaranteed probation as a worst-case scenario, especially because there was no weapon. Nick and I showed up to every court date and Hurk's lawyer was right. The state couldn't pay that snitch or any witness to testify. Hurk was set to be processed and released any day.

"Yo Dee, you sure you wanna build a spot by Hope way?" asked Nick as we sat at a red light on Orleans Street.

"Doesn't matter where we hustle. No beef and no killing is all I really care about. We can sell drugs until our arms fall off and cops don't care but when the murders come..."

Skrrrrrrrrrr! BOOM!

A blue pickup slammed into the back of our car, making Nick's head slap the steering wheel like a crash dummy. His neck made a popping sound. I unbuckled my safety belt and reached over.

"Yo, what the fuck, you good, are you dead?"

His nod answered my question. I hopped out to see what the fuck was wrong with the dudes in the pickup. Two pint-sized Mexicans hopped out and charged toward me as if it was our fault. They could hardly speak English and probably didn't really want any trouble, so I flashed the pistol strapped to my belt. They took off running in opposite directions, leaving their truck.

Nick didn't have insurance and our windows had limo tint. We also had pistols on us and the car was a bong on wheels, so I dragged Nick out.

"Yo, forget this car. We leavin' this crap, I'ma buy you a new one." I said as my buck-sixty frame tried to support Nick's 220 pounds of jewelry, acne, baby fat, and empty chicken boxes.

Three hours later, Nick lay across the couch still, his pudgy hands covering his face. I tried to pull one off but wasn't strong enough. Tears trickled under his palms as he said, "Dee, go see Discoooo. Get me something, my back. Yo please, God, ehhhh."

Disco Joe was a recovering addict who now worked as a nurse's assistant or aide or something. Her place was over on the other end of Castle Street, right off of Jefferson. Disco offered "ghetto healthcare" to street dudes like us. You could get bullet or stab wounds stitched, random shots, and STD cures.

Nick was right, Disco Joe would have some pain pills or something for his back so I rolled him a blunt and went to her place.

When I arrived, she was sprawled across her stoop, Newport balanced on her bottom lip, with cloudy diamond and gold rings on all ten of her fingers that looked like brass knuckles.

"Disco, wuz up, baby, I need some pain pills for Nick. We just crushed his whip."

"I got Tylox, Oxys, or Perks, baby," replied Disco with that half-lit cigarette that just wouldn't fall. She resembled an anorexic Mary J. Blige with a hustle that never stopped moving. Disco made money hand over fist and her shop rocked 24/7.

"What you think I should buy him?"

"Two hundred fifty Perks for fifteen hundred dollars for you, bae, and tell ya sexy-ass uncle I wanna dig all in his ass," replied Disco as she licked the crust off of the edge of her bottom lip, cigarette still holding on for dear life.

I ignored the invite and cashed her out. She brought the pills out in three long tangerine colored, white-capped cylinders, "I tossed a bundle of Tylox in there too, on me," she said as I examined the bag and jumped off her top step.

"Why you givin' me free stuff?"

"Cuz I love you, bae, and Bip was my bae too, you know that!" I said thanks, blew her a kiss, and headed straight home.

My Nextel hadn't gone off in a while, which was weird because it's normally a hotline, so I checked it and saw that it was on silent. Two missed calls from Nick and twenty from Uncle Gee. Twenty calls—I can't take another death, I thought as I hit the callback key.

"Nephew! What the fuck iz up?" said Gee on the other end.

Gee used to be the man in east Baltimore but now he's hit or miss. He flashes money when he's clean and robs everybody in sight as soon as that monkey climbs back on him.

"I'm chillin', man, what's good?"

"I'ma come see you later, man, I need you, for real."

I told him to come through around midnight. Nick should be good by then. I knew Gee wanted something. I could always see right through that "I need you, I love you" bullshit.

Gee coming by could be a good thing. I thought I could whole-sale him some of that heroin and use the cash to buy Nick a nice car. He wanted a black Lexus GS 300 and I could get that for him and something for me without touching my cash or the coke.

On the walk home, I pondered on the fact that there was no perfect drug strip or situation for us to enter this game. The key is to buy low and sell high any and everywhere you can. I was over thinking this kingpin shit. Those drugs should've been gone. I didn't have a real drug connect or a reason to babysit all of that product, plus Nick and I could've died today—fuck that. It was time to move all of it.

Back home, I used all of my power to sit Nick up.

"Nick, listen to me, bro. Chew three of these joints and you will be good. I'ma chew some too," I said while putting the pills in his hand. He ate all three of them and eased back in the chair.

"Yo, dey taste like shit and baby powder mixed!" said Nick with a twisted face.

"How you know what baby powder and shit taste like?" I replied as I swallowed mine and washed it back with a swig of Belvedere. "Drink some of this too."

I know alcohol makes Percocets work better—they go together like apples and cinnamon—shit, I don't even know anyone who would take Perks without yak. I once heard that Percocets worked faster when chewed. I'm not sure about that, but moments later,

Nick crawled over to the corner of the living room and balled up like an angry fist. There he farted, yawned, and slipped into euphoria with his eyes open, a little drool wetting his chin.

I called Hope and told her that I'd be visiting her tomorrow with a special surprise. Then I had to pull the dope out of the safe before Gee got there. He didn't need to know about everything. Tomorrow was going to be a great day, I thought as I closed and locked the red door. I'm giving Hope three thousand dollars, getting Nick a car, Hurk could be a free man, I'm putting my uncle back in the game, and I'll be teeing out my own crack in a few different blocks over east.

The pill in me was growing and then glowing. Bright lights and soft memories fogged my thoughts. Everything became easy in an instant. Those little pills were instant—instant gratification.

"Dee, get the fuck up! Boy, you lifted," said Nick, standing over top of me with perfect posture. I never saw a person with a straighter back.

"Yo, how you feel, Nick," I said while wiping drool off of my own chin.

"Amazing," said Nick repeatedly as he threw jabs at the air in Ali motions. He shadowboxed for like ten minutes and then finally told me Gee called and would be here in five minutes. I looked at my watch and couldn't believe that I had just slept for seven hours. What a pill—I think I like them.

I washed the high off of my face and wrapped Gee's half brick up in a pillowcase. I then told Nick to go out and get some baking soda, a bag of ice, and some bottles of aspirin because I'd be cooking later.

As Nick was going out, Gee came walking in. They dapped each other up as Nick said, "I'll see y'all lata."

"Dee, what's up, how you feel?" said Gee as he walked in and surveyed the place. His eyes looked like clots. He smelled like a gallon of Hennessy and Popeye's beans and rice.

"I'm holdin' on, missin' Bip, but hey," I replied, trying not to break eye contact.

Gee then went into a story about how special Bip was and that I'm lucky to have spent those last days with him. He called us the best things that ever happened to him. I wasn't sure if it was love or our ability to support him financially that got him talking that way—either way, it felt good to talk to a relative.

"Gee, Bip left me a half brick of dope. It looks really good and I'll give it to you for twenty racks even though it's worth a lot more."

"I ain't got shit, man, and I owe some people," he replied, without blinking. His desperation stunk.

"Well, what do you have? I know you don't think I'm frontin' you a whole joint. I ain't Scarface."

"Yeah, boy but you ain't no drug dealer neither. Fuck you gonna do with that?"

Gee didn't know. Shit, I didn't know, but realistically I'm probably not going back to college. I'm in the game now.

"Oh, Gee, I definitely hustle now. I just don't wanna fuck with dope, it's too complicated. Crack man, I'm a crack man."

I had Nick as my general, and we bump Jay Z all day so "Rockafella" would be my stamp. After tomorrow I'd have a rack of clients and maintaining that, or at least building that, would mean no freebies, even to family.

Gee walked over to our couch and sunk into the center. His 250-pound frame made the cushions fold up like a V. I leaned my back against the wall and slid down to the floor. Gee had a look on his face. The kind of look people get right before they ask a really stupid question.

"Gee, what you want from me, man? Like for real."

"I'm tryin' to get that whole thing from you, boy, I can move all of it. I'm good for it, boy I'm ya—"

I cut in and told him that I wasn't even listening to that "I'm your family" shit, "you my nephew" shit. As far as he knew that's all I had, and I wasn't going to give him a chance to fuck that up.

"Why you hit me for help anyway? How you know I could look out? I don't have a job."

Gee said he wasn't thinking drugs, he was thinking cash. He knew Bip had a bunch of it, probably left it to me, and he just thought he could borrow some buy-money and get us all right.

The whole story made sense except for the fact that he owed Bip cash from back in 1996 when he was supposed to be in rehab but checked out early, relapsed and begged for money every day. Bip would mock him like, "I need helpppppp, y'all livinnnnnn, this shit is fuckin me upppp!" He lent Gee 10K when he came out of rehab and would always crack jokes on how Gee would probably never pay him back.

"I'll give you ten stacks and the rest when I get back in town. You a tough muh-fucker man. Got damn!"

I said no and told him to give me fifteen now and nine when he got back since he didn't have all of the money up front—that was my final offer. I knew that he could easily make a ton after paying his workers and me so I had to add that extra tax. If he wasn't family, I wouldn't have fronted him shit. We shook on it and I told him that he could pick it up tomorrow or whenever he had that fifteen on him.

Nick came back about hour after Gee left. He stopped and got some chicken cheesesteaks but I didn't eat. I was too excited and ready to work. Beating that extra money out of Gee ignited something inside of me, something I had never felt before. I grabbed the bag of supplies that I asked Nick to get and laid them across our countertop.

My Pyrex was big enough to cook a whole bird so making an eighth would be really easy. I wiped down the counter with a warm cloth. Everything was clean and clear. In front of me was a Pyrex of boiling water, a cloud of mist, a few ice cubes, a box of Arm & Hammer, a sack of cocaine, a pitcher of Kool-Aid, a cup of vodka, and bunch of opportunity. I never really cooked before but I saw it done at least a million times, so I knew I could do it. I was hard-wired for this.

I dumped the coke on top of the boiling water—and watched the oil set up. I looked to left, to right. Nick forgot the aspirin—fuck!

"Nick, you forgot the FUCKIN' aspirin," I yelled, busting a lung.

Giving out high quality testers is the most important part of being a great dealer. You have to build that hype like in any other industry. It introduces your product to the world. As I explained to Nick plenty of times: you don't need aspirin to cook crack but adding it makes the rocks burn slower, giving fiends the illusion that their high is lasting longer than the standard eleven minutes.

I had to think quickly or risk fucking the batch up, so I blasted up to the medicine cabinet . . . nothing but toothpaste and Proactiv gel for Nick's acne. The Tylox!

"I'm running to get aspirin now, Yo, my bad!" shouted Nick as he fell out the front door. I smashed up the small pills and sprinkled the powder into the pot. Baking soda came next; I whipped it hard with my right hand and quickly tossed the ice chips in with my left. The end result was golden—similar to the color of Kellogg's Corn Pops.

It was a little darker than what I was used to, but almost half more than I started with, and the fumes smelled right, a little funky, but right. Cutting it with Tylox could be genius or a fuck-up—I guessed I'd see tomorrow.

Nick came back in with a bag full of Motrin. I told him that he was too late and the batch was done—oh, and I asked what was up with the Motrin? Together Nick and I capped up a nation of crack samples. Two bitty shaved rocks in bottle after bottle. Our tops were black and we were ready. We were bringing a whole new element to the street and the pressure was off because I didn't pay for the product. I could afford to fuck up a batch or two.

I fixed us some cups of vodka and continued capping. Our little black-topped bottles covered the table. Vials are deceiving, just like the crack inside. Crack is this over-hyped drug that fucks up lives and makes people crazy in exchange for an eleven-minute high. Vials are magnifying glasses that make it seem like you are getting more drugs. You aren't. They both promise more while giving less.

"Ah, Dee, one day we'll have naked bitches baggin' up for us like Nino Brown at the Carter and shit," said Nick.

"Man, you watch too much TV." I told Nick that I knew there were three target areas where we could sample this stuff other than Hope's block, including Highlandtown, Latrobe, and 21st. He had a few spots as well and we had more than enough product. We capped up about a ounce of testers, as we call them, and almost a quarter brick of nicks and dimes.

"After we tee to other niggas, I'm a find us a block too. We gonna get our own spot, man," said Nick, making his way over to the couch.

Nick popped two Perks and fell asleep. I ate one and walked around the neighborhood. I stopped at Bocek Park and thought back to the days when my dirt bike ripped through the grass there and my only concern was being the best rider. I sat there in my state of Percocet-driven nostalgia and faded into the shadows. I loved the park at night. It's consistent—pitch black and empty and remains that way until dawn, every day.

ROCKAFELLA

I called my boy Carlos the cab driver and told him that we needed him from seven a.m. until a little past noon. He's tall and dark-skinned with huge white teeth that always smile at you. His cab was as clean as his grill. No trash, no smell, and really no evidence of customers. Los had always been a neat freak since we were kids, with creases in his school uniform khakis draping over scuffless shell-toe Adidas.

It didn't take long for our scent to stink his cab up.

"Damn, y'all ain't playin', huh? I knew y'all ain't smoking so I bet y'all got a bunch to sell!" said Carlos, peering through the rearview.

I tossed him three hundred dollars and named our destinations. The conversations I had with the dealers from each area were identical: "Yo, I'm giving samples out for your best customers so hit me later and let me know if you want some." I played Little League with most of the young dealers and the rest of them knew Bip or Nick. We rode around to make Nick's drop-offs as well and picked up the cash from Gee. I told him that he could pick up his half brick after I counted the money. He said, "Only because you are you. Anybody else wouldn't touch the money until I touched the product." I told Carlos our last stop was Seth's Auto in Dundalk.

Heading to buy a car, Carlos said, "Damn, Dee, new whips, Yo, wassup? Throw a nigga some work, boy. You know I got kids and shit."

"Oh yeah, how's Kyra?" I asked. Kyra was Carlos's lady and elementary school sweetheart.

"Kyra's fucked up and wantin' money, nigga, throw me some work!"

I told Carlos that we were building and I could probably fit him in somewhere.

One thing that gave me pause is that Carlos had a rep for being a shooter. Uncle Gee is a shooter, and Hurk—he's the shooter of all shooters. I have no interest in murder. I'm not into that homicide life at all. Hustling and committing murders doesn't work—you have to pick a side. I understand that the two worlds can't exist with each other, in Baltimore anyway. I was determined to not war with anyone. Death hurts and I've seen too many. I had enough shooters around me, but I liked Carlos so I tried to figure something out.

A whole line of dirty pearl and rusty-gold broken-down Acuras were spread across the front of Seth's Auto.

"Dee, what's this the lemon factory and shit. These buckets beat," said Nick while observing the lot.

I told him that the good cars were in the back, and if nothing was good enough, Seth could take us to the auction. Seth buzzed us in. His office was a trailer without wheels, packed tight and made out of paperwork—paperwork on the desk, paperwork busting out of the file cabinets, overflowing with folders. His lot looked cheap as his suit but he was loaded. Seth gets cars for everybody who is anybody. Big-time guys get 600 Benzes and 700 series Beamers. Real big guys get Bentleys and vehicles that we can't even pronounce. He had a couple of E Class Benzes and some Lexus ES 300s that looked pretty fresh and in our pay grade.

"Hey, Dee, glad you stopped by," said Seth with both arms

extended. His nose owned his face and was probably the only nose in the world strong enough to hold up the set of thick frames he had on.

"No disrespect but I'm not a hugger," I replied as I opted for a handshake. Nick had eased off to check out the rest of the inventory.

"So what are you looking for? Benz, Lexus, I just got a nice Rover in. Wait, is your car still on hold?"

"I don't know. I don't even want it back. I'm just lookin' for a GS for Nick and I don't even know what I wanna drive yet. I do want something nice, though, eventually."

Seth asked me how much I wanted to spend. I told him that it depended on the car. He then said that his friend had a nice 1996 black-on-black GS 300 over on Belair Road.

Nick leaped in front of me. "Dat's me, how much, unk?"

Seth pulled out his cell to get a price check. I wasn't going to let my friend ride around in a '96. I told Nick that he needed to chill when doing business with car dealers because most of them are spineless rats, including Seth. I didn't care if Seth looked out for Bip or any other street dude, he still wanted to make as much money as possible, like any other hustler. Excited people like Nick always fall victim to the "ignorance tax." A guy like Seth smells your ignorance, so they tax you! Car dealers, lawyers, and payday loan crooks are notorious for this.

"Okay, guys, follow me," said Seth. We walked around back to an emerald green GS 400 with tan leather. Nick was speechless.

"How much for that?" I asked, poker face on.

"That's a '01 with about twenty thousand miles. I need at least thirty-two thousand and that's because you are such a great guy."

"Naw, fuck that! That's too much," said a frustrated Nick. I told him to chill again.

"Nick, take a walk, man, lemme holler at Seth."

I told him that I was flat broke but I'm about to make a run and that we were goin' to be doing a lot of business.

"Dee, make me an offer. A good one."

"I got twenty-three thousand cash, in the bag. And I'ma buy another car like next week. Let us take it."

Seth paused for a minute, let out a deep breath, looked at his feet, and then tossed me the keys. He said I'd owe him a big one. I thanked him and told a now gleaming Nick to cash him out.

"Yo, you gotta new GS now, boy, it's on!" yelled Nick with face pressed against the driver's side window, admiring the interior and caressing the side of the car.

"Naw," I said. "You have a new GS. I said this was for you. I wanna thank you for holding me down!"

Nick flipped, turned around and squeezed the wind out of my chest in one motion; he was so excited that he dropped the open bag of cash on the ground. We calmed him down and did the paperwork. Seth had a fictitious company set up with license numbers and a real insurance policy. We just had to endorse the documents and screw on the sixty-day cardboard temporary tag.

Fifteen minutes later and we were cruising on Route 40, headed back down the hill. Nick was at the wheel with a low Orioles brim. His seat leaned back far enough to touch the rear chair. I checked my phone. Thirty missed calls—a few random girls, five from Gee who wanted his work, and about twenty from Hope. I tried to call her back but got no answer.

"Yo, Nick, you got a strap, right?"

"Always, what's wrong?" he replied.

"Okay, stop by Hope's, Yo."

PROTECTOR

I called Hope again when we were about five minutes away. She answered on the first ring.

"He hit me and I'm bleeding, can you come and get me, please, Dee?" was all she said before hanging up. I couldn't get a word in. I pulled my pistol off of my waist, and sat it on my lap.

"Yo, Brock slapped Hope, split her shit too," I said as I popped the clip in and out of the gun.

"Why she wit his li'l ugly ass anyway? Ellwood, right?"

"Right," I replied as Nick parked about a half block away from her house. I told him to stand by the back door just in case he tried to run. I walked around front and tried her door—it was open. I held my weapon and slowly crept up to their apartment.

Knock knock knock . . .

"Go away, I fuckin' hate you!" came from the opposite side of the door.

"Naw, it's me, Dee!" I said, tucking the pistol.

She opened the door. He had left her face all lumpy and red. Her skin was puffy and bruised, covered by a mangled head of hair. I couldn't tell where the tears stopped or the blood started.

"Yo, pack some clothes and come with me," I said.

Frantically she started throwing some of her things into a trash bag as I waited. Brock came in through the front door laughing

49

and headed up the steps. I opened their apartment door and stood behind it.

"Hope, baby. Ha ha, I love you, girl, where you at?"

He walked in and shut the door, and my pistol met his face. He raised both of his hands straight over his head.

"Chill, Dee. Hold up, what's goin' on?" said Brock as he backed up into the wall.

"Get on your fuckin' knees. Hope, hurry up!" I shouted as I patted Brock down and checked him for a weapon.

Hope saw me holding the pistol and dropped the bag.

"Oh my God, what are you doing? STOP!"

I spun around. "Get your shit Hope!"

Brock grabbed the gun and we tussled. My hands locked on it but I couldn't pull it away; he was three times stronger than me. We hit a wall and knocked some stuff on the floor. Nick ran in and slapped him across the head with his gun. All three of us fell, but only Nick and I got up. I rolled him over.

"Hold his face!"

Nick put him in a chokehold, similar to the ones that cops sometimes used on us, and angled his face in my direction. I gathered myself and gave him a series of pistol-saps across the mouth, enough to cause a splatter on my sneaks and tee. Hope's screams narrated the beating. Nick pulled me off. Hope said something about calling the cops, and Nick yelled, "Nigga, she buggin', let's book." I didn't say a word. I just ran down the steps behind Nick, jetted up the block and hopped in his car.

"Fuck is up with her? Callin' the cops on us and he split her shit, dat's dumb," said Nick as we rode up Madison. I told him to stop at the CC's Carryout so I could grab some more vials. I dialed her number and it went straight to voice mail. We hit CC's five minutes later. Todd from Greenmount—one of the dealers I gave samples to—was standing in the doorway when I exited the car.

"Todd, wassup, man?"

"Nigga, you wassup!" he replied. "Nigga, you that nigga!"

He went on to say that Rockafella was the best crack that he had ever sampled in his life. Junkies who hit it were dancing, rejoicing, throwing up, racing all over the street, and begging for more all day. They even told their junkie friends who told their junkie friends. His block must have looked like a casting call for "Thriller."

And it wasn't just Todd, everybody was looking for me all day, and he wanted to buy ten thousand dollars' worth of whatever I could get him that night. Nick and I had three more similar conversations on the way back to the house. East Baltimore had gone Rockafella crazy that quick.

"Yo, we about to jam," I told Nick as he parked in front of our crib. A lanky silhouette materialized from the alley. "D.O.C." was tatted across a gray sweatshirt that approached our car. Nick reached for his gun but I stopped him—Hurk was back.

We bear-hugged. He couldn't have been freed at a better time. He didn't have to hide anymore and we had the best shit in the city, or at least in east Baltimore, anyway. Nick made Hurk test-drive his car through downtown. Hurk was ready to talk business and said that he wasn't going back to jail. He said that his reckless days were far behind him. Nick was eager to tell Hurk about my cooking skills. I just called Hope over and over again but no answer— straight to voice mail every time.

"So what can I do, Dee? I'm ready to work tonight," said Hurk. I didn't want him to do too much in the city because he was scorching hot. His rap about never going back to prison was cool but words are just words—you had to show me.

We rode back to my house and I immediately went to work. I cooked the other half brick that I had pulled out the previous day while Nick and Hurk sliced and capped crack rocks until their fingers bled. Gee came by and picked up his work.

I called Hope one more time. The phone rang but she still didn't pick up. I wasn't sure why she was ignoring me; maybe she was angry. I just wanted to help and I felt like I did the right thing. She'll come around, I thought, before I popped two Perks. One was really good, two felt like new pussy, or money—no, two felt like real love.

ASHLAND AND MADEIRA

Now I needed a spot to push this stuff. A nation, a place to call home. Ashland and Madeira was the first spot that popped in my mind. A bunch of different crews had acquired and lost Ashland and Madeira over the last ten years. Street fortunes were made and lost there. My uncle Gee had it for the longest.

The highlight of my week back as a twelve-year-old in middle school was riding my little PW50 through there to kick it with him. A collage of forty-plus hustlers and countless junkies flooded his corner until you couldn't tell who was selling what. They screamed the names of different products and prices like Wall Street bankers—with Gee running it all, squeezing a half-empty bottle of Hennessy and wads of cash poking out of his pockets.

"Uncle Gee, what's good?" I'd say, parking the bike by the curb, dapping his workers.

"Nephew, sit and shut up, you need to hear this!" he'd reply before going deep into some story on how he was fucking with two of the three members from TLC or how he put a guy's head in a car door before closing it—and always how the money would continue to flow through Ashland and Madeira.

After the rants came handouts. Sometimes he'd hit me with a small bundle of tens and twenties that I'd stuff in my socks, then he'd wrap a tight blunt and I'd chill on the corner for hours, blowing weed with Gee and the rest of the big dogs.

He made money, lots of it, but the place suffered from unorganized shifts, dealers fistfighting in the midst of sales, junkies being fucked in cars without tinted windows while us schoolkids watched, crack fiends with crack babies everywhere, long-ass dope lines, heavy overdosing, barefoot children, and terrified residents. It was the true definition of an open-air drug market.

Cops would pull up in vans and arrest twenty to thirty people at a time. It was easy for them because all of the crime was transparent and out in the open. The dealers sat on stoops next to half-empty forty-ounces of Olde English with pockets full of cash and drugs—no stash, no system, no strategy.

And then there were the shootouts.

I almost got my head blown off on Ashland Avenue a number of times. Crown Vics and Chevy Corsicas would roll up on us; automatic weapons would tilt out of the windows and blast. Gee and his goons would bust back while me and the rest of kids would scatter like roaches under a flicked light, diving under cars and balling up in between stoops. This didn't happen every day, but it did happen enough for us to develop a routine. I'm still leery of limo tints and cars that drive past me with their headlights off at night.

My uncle's temper made the block a war zone. He was always slapping someone or shooting. Shooting to boost name, shooting for territory, or shooting just to shoot. A lot of rival crews wanted Gee's head and we all knew that, but despite the obvious danger, I still came around, all the way up until Cherry was shot in 1993.

Cherry was one of Gee's workers. He was a skinny slick talker with a big face, who was always going on about moving to Atlanta to start a family and a business. We'd laugh, like "Nigga, you a going nowhere!" and he wasn't. We all knew that Cherry spent his money before he made it.

Cherry may have bluffed on moving away but he didn't bluff on friendship. He lent cash to anyone, took shorts from fiends who was always a buck or two short, and protected his boys. Cherry covered Gee midway through one of those drive-by shootouts and caught one in the chest. He spun around and landed facefirst on the concrete. We ran up on him as the shooters sped off.

"Cherry, you good? Get up!" I yelled. His cousin Li'l Bo flipped him and propped his head. Cherry spoke, and blood came out. Li'l Bo yelled for help. It wasn't the first time I saw a murder, but it was the first time I felt one. My heart dropped past my sneakers. A crowd had formed. I guessed the ambulance drivers were on break because minutes flew past without sirens.

I saw Cherry and me hooping the other day. I saw us sharing sunflower seeds; I spit the shells out, he chewed and swallowed them, and I told him that was weird. We had both stood on line for Air Jordan 3 Retros a week before. I saw my uncle putting him in the headlock and us laughing. We were friends. Ten years or more apart but we were the same. I looked at him lying on that ground and saw myself spitting that blood up, gurgling on it as it wrapped my chin and spilled down my neck.

"Get him out the street!" Gee ordered. We hovered around his body and picked him up; blood soaked our t-shirts and stained our jeans. We laid him on the sidewalk by Mrs. Gina's house. She squeezed her grandbabies, biting her lip, covering their eyes. Sirens pulled up a few minutes too late. RIP Cherry.

I indirectly learned everything I needed to know about hustling from chilling around them. I knew my block would look nothing like the shit my uncle ran.

MY BLOCK

My wholesale game was intact because of the weight I had sold off to some other crews, and now it was time for me to rebuild Ashland and Madeira. I didn't even have to fight anyone. The block was completely vacant—a bunch of dudes had slaughtered each other or got locked up or found Jesus. Either way, I slid right in.

The first time we handed out testers was on a Sunday. Hurk, Nick, and I had been putting the word out all over east Baltimore, letting all the fiends know that we birthed Rockafella, had the best ready-rock, and would be giving away jumbo tester's. Most dudes only sampled off of the residue from their Pyrex, but I inherited this, so it was only right that I gave away the good stuff.

8:00 a.m.
I popped up and drove to Pete's Grill on Greenmount. A bunch of turkey sausage, some eggs and cheese, and a rack of pancakes is what I carried out. The day was going to be huge and I couldn't have anybody hungry. Everybody was awake when I got back to the house. Nick eyed the bag of food so hard as I crossed the room, you'd think a naked chick was in there.

We inhaled our breakfast. I threw on a new white tee and thought about sneakers. My room was a sneaker gallery. I'd been in the shoe game forever and had thousands and thousands of dollars in boxed Jordans and untouched Barkleys. My sneaker collection might have cost more than a Harvard education. I had bags and bags of Dope-Dealers, or Dopes, which were Nike Foamposites, Rockport boots, or any shoe costing two hundred dollars or more. The logic was that you'd have to be selling dope to afford shoes like that. Silver Duncans would be good for the day.

10:00 a.m.
Hurk banged the horn as Nick I came out. Project Pat ripped through the speakers. We were really about to be the young boys on top. Hurk had the samples tucked in a JanSport. I hopped in the back and we cruised up Ashland Avenue.

10:15 a.m.
We had to circle the block and come back. I had left my pistol. I'd leave my glasses, I could leave my coat, hoodie, or my sweater but I wasn't leaving my gun. I tucked my .45 by my waistline and hopped back in Hurk's car. We rode up Ashland Avenue until we hit Madeira and parked a block away. A real hustler should always park at least one block away.

10:30 a.m.
A line of fiends gathered well before showtime. They were a diverse group of scabby-faced muthafuckers, nine-to-fivers, some whites, some single moms, absent fathers, ex–ball players, bus drivers, fat junkies (which I don't understand), and church niggas. Hurk leaned on a lamppole that was about as thin as he was, dangled an aluminum bat over his left shoulder, and locked eyes on the crowd. Nick climbed on top of someone's Honda and yelled, "Tees of that shit! The best shit out chea hoe!" He lifted the JanSport well above

his head. Some children looked on in awe even though they knew what was up as old women watched from their stoops in despair.

"Get in a single-file line! Get in a straight line or y'all ain't g'ttin' shit!" I shouted. They were like kids, happy kids, because we had their candy.

11:00 a.m.
Nick dug his hand deep into the bag, gripped a handful of vials, and whaled them into the sky. Rockafella rained on the bunch. Rocks hit the concrete, bounced off the curb, fell into hands and everywhere. Customers dove into the concrete. They fought and stepped all over each other for loose vials. A dude in a post office uniform headlocked a woman. Hurk leaped off the pole and cracked his back with the bat.

"Chill, bitch!" yelled Hurk, cracking him again. "Let the lady get some!"

The dude howled like he was giving birth. Another blow across the back of his head silenced the screams. No one else acted up after that, they got their free samples and were back in minutes to cop.

11:15 a.m.
And just that quick, Ashland and Madeira went from being dried up to flooded with crack money.

A DRUG CREW

Sometimes the lines wrapped the corner, and we had to move them into the alley to shift attention away from the front of the block. We couldn't cut and cap fast enough. Our pockets and socks couldn't contain the cash. Me, Nick, and Hurk couldn't run Madeira Street on our own. Sure we could move weight and run small operations, but I had a lot of drugs to sell. I needed a few good men who wanted some dough and were down to earn it.

Now, don't let TV shows and hood movies lead you to believe that drug crews only consist of childhood friends with crackhead parents who came up poor in some housing projects and, frustrated with their living situation by the age of sixteen, so they decide to be kingpins. And don't let the news fool you into believing that we are all bloodthirsty killers who only sell dope and stay ready to shoot shit up. Fox and MSNBC and CNN like to portray us as B-roll footage of skinny teens in sweat suits with gold teeth and AK's. That's not the case, either. It doesn't work like that. A hustler staff could include eight-year-old kids who play with Ninja Turtle dolls, awkward teens, Comcast employees who hate their shift managers, mothers who really want to find work but can't, grandmas raising three generations of kids at the same time, asshole cops, the prettiest girl from your high school, the Little League basketball coach, for sure, city workers who want a little something extra at the end of the week, junkies, and basically anyone else who seems loyal—because you can never really tell.

Everybody has a breaking point, and even dudes who have been tested fold. A stranger could take thirty years for you while your best friend is in the next room ratting, crying, gargling on his own snot while explaining the whole operation. The no-snitching thing is a façade, and it's evident when you look at the incarceration rates. The street-corner retention ratio is too low to be building lifelong relationships and unbreakable bonds—y'all could be on today and off tomorrow. I'd even argue that it's better to work with strangers just in case you have to throw them out of a window one day. Who would you rather throw out of a window—some Comcast nigga or your childhood best friend?

I know Gee ran through multiple crews and Bip had a new clique like every two months. It wasn't about being a real friend or a fake one—it's just that jail and death were guaranteed and you had to survive. You had to focus on you.

Selling dope is a team game on the surface but you're really alone. The game is like dodge ball—you start with a team and you want to protect them but that's not always the case as things move along. People will be hit, and finishing with the cast that you started with is a rarity. You really have to be able to stand on your own in the mist of the ten, twenty, fifty employees and friends that surround you every day. Some quit and some expire but the game doesn't give a shit. Losing friends hurts and thick skin is needed. There are no therapists on the street and pain is only mended with music, sex, pills, yak, weed, and the shit that we were out there selling.

But by a month in I had a solid team of seven: Nick, Li'l Bo, Tone, Fat Tay, Young Block, Miss Angie, and Dog Boy.

TONE, DOG BOY, AND US

Tone: AA Male, forty-something years old, maybe fifty.
Occupation: Shooter, meaning he'll shoot you.
Salary: $400 a week plus room and board.

I don't know where I found Tone at. He was known in this hood or that hood for the same things, which was talking a whole bunch of shit and then backing it up, being trigger-happy and never having any picks or choices—he'd go to war with anyone.

He didn't care if you were a beat cop or a known gangsta— he'd run you down, put three in your dome, and then piss on you in broad daylight. I was lucky to have him on our side. And if he thought you were telling, he'd get you too.

Tone would stare out of the second-floor window on North Madeira Street with a shredded toothpick in his mouth and a raised eyebrow. He was like my guardian angel because he had the drop on everyone. His skin was all nasty and discolored and spotted like a leopard, mostly from the years of heroin and prison. All of his veins were dry and shriveled up. Disco Joe had to show me how to shoot him up with dope so that he could work. I used to strangle his ankle with a tourniquet until the little veins popped out, from there I'd pump him with enough heroin to get through his day.

Sunup till sundown he sat in the window with a sawed-off

shotgun resting on his chest like a newborn. Handguns lay on his coffee table, ammo filled his sock drawer, and he had no fear in his heart. Rob my workers, and get your head knocked off by him.

Li'l Bo: AA male, seventeen.
Occupation: The Money Man.
Salary: $750 a week on average.

Li'l Bo had a slick face and slicker walk; he was just slick in general.

He was Cherry's little cousin. I used to fuck wide-ass Wanda on Lakewood back in middle school and Li'l Bo had the big sister, who had a wide ass too. We've been friends and plugging each other with girls ever since, so it was only right that I hit him up when I grabbed the block.

I trusted Li'l Bo with the money because he was never a hater. He didn't talk shit when he saw me in nice cars or badmouth me when we were fucking the same girls. Li'l Bo once said the idea of hating made his mouth ache—I agreed. He had faith in himself, meaning that he could stand seeing others shine, even when he wasn't. Li'l Bo would hide stacks of cash in a Mickey D's bag by the trash can on the corner, have bundles tucked by his nuts, stacks in his socks and puffed all in his jeans. He was stick bony but the bulky cash make his pants look like he had an erection and child-bearing hips.

Li'l Bo collected the cash from customers, stashed it, and then signaled Fat Tay the amount of drugs that the customer was supposed to receive. Signals changed hourly—they were head taps or nose rubs or hand gestures or a combination of all, making up a hood sign language only we could decode. Li'l Bo collected cash all day. And since Li'l Bo handled the bread, he never, ever touched drugs under any circumstances, because cops can take all of your cash if they can prove that it's drug related.

Fat Tay: AA Male, thirty-five but looks forty.
Occupation: Hitter, a person who controls the ground stash.
Salary: Depends on how I felt or if he showed up.

I hate Fat Tay. He's sloppy in both stature and work ethic. He's built like a bowling pin with feet and has small, perky breasts that are visible in everything he wears, even his coats. Tay's grown, looks grown, and dates high school girls. They don't like him— they lack fathers. He fills that void and buys them all of the shit that they don't need.

Li'l Bo talked me into hiring Fat Tay because they are first cousins, so I employed him as my hitter. Hitters are disposable like pawns or those infantry dudes they throw into the line of fire. Tay kept dimes of ready tucked in the inside of tennis balls we bounced off of the brick walls that surrounded us, loose vials in paper bags near the trash, more crack in the rusty downspouts, and some more loose capped vials of crack stuffed in Tay's big fat ass. His ass held a lot of crack. It was like a mini fridge. Most cops didn't want to check there but the fiends didn't care if their glass bottles were smeared with shit from Tay's ass—they just wanted to get high. Tay's job wasn't always held by Tay. Sometimes kids would do it, sometimes junkies do it, and, really, anyone who wanted to make a couple. It was really easy to find hitters because the job required zero trust or skill.

Dog Boy: AA Male, maybe twelve, who knows.
Occupation: Lookout.
Salary: $100 here, $100 there, and new kicks.

Dog Boy was best friends with my little cousin Scola. They were equally learning disabled, loved Power Rangers—the red one to be exact—and both enjoyed eating lead paint chips. Most of the kids where I come from, including myself, loved to eat lead paint chips. You can peel them right off of the wall and they are sweet and sticky like taffy. You can have as many sweet sticky chips as you like because they are everywhere and free and you don't have to ask your parents for them.

Dog Boy had got a big forty-thousand-dollar check from eating paint chips—he fucked every penny up on the hood. Everybody got new dirt bikes, Polo, and Hilfiger.

Many think Dog Boy got his name from his appearance—he looks like a bald adult shih tzu with clipped ears attached to an adolescent body—but that's just a coincidence. We call him Dog Boy because before he was our lookout, he used to walk dogs for some big-time dealers that got snatched by the feds. I didn't know his name so I just started calling him Dog Boy and it stuck. Sometimes he calls me Pops. Years of lead paint poison made him answer questions with delayed responses, but he was on point when the cops rushed.

"Yerooooooo," was our signal for cops. "One time yeroooo!" Dog Boy would bark when the knockers struck. That signal sparked our runner.

Young Block: AA Male, sixteen years old.
Occupation: Runner, the guy who moves the cash from the block to our stash.
Salary: $750 a week.

Young Block was the runner. He'd grab the cash and get it back to our house a few blocks away. Didn't matter if cops were coming or not, he always made sure we didn't have too much cash lying around. Block ran like he had four thighs; he was the fastest kid in east Baltimore.

Block never spoke. His name was TayQuan but one day Li'l Bo said that he was young and stuck on the block so we started calling him Young Block. His mom is Lena and she's stuck too. She used to be pretty and employed but drug addiction had swallowed her face. She'd come by the corner once or twice a day when Block wasn't around. She'd fake like she was looking for him but she wasn't.

"Deeeeeeeeee," she'd whine to me. "Where my son? Can you help me out till my check come?" Her check never came. Not to me, anyway, but I had to help her. She was going to get high regardless and I couldn't have Block's mom out sucking dick for crack money or stealing, so I'd have Fat Tay toss her two or three pills. And I'd do the same for his mom.

The last, maybe most important, member of our operation was Miss Angie. She was like everybody's aunt.

Miss Angie: AA female, fifty-something.
Occpation: Cook.
Pay: Grocery, cigarette, lotto, favors, and church money.

Miss Angie wasn't really a part of our crew but she was. She'd been living on Madeira Street for a thousand years and was basically just a helpless resident. She'd seen crews before us and would probably see crews after us.

I took a liking to her because she was a hustler too, just like us. She'd tell us all about her church and Jesus and then try to sell us chicken dinners. Selling drugs all day definitely builds up an appetite and her dinners actually were delicious. Her house smelled like old people, ass, and mothballs. She had a big picture of white Jesus on her wall. I kept telling her Jesus was black but she didn't listen.

"If Jesus was black, then why he white on all these pictures, Dee! Riddle me that!"

"Cuz white people want you to associate them with God. That nigga was black, I'm tellin' you! Hair like wool! That's a Jheri Curl!"

Eventually I ignored the painting because her cooking was better than eating chicken boxes and pizza every day, plus she always made a vegetable. And even though her vegetables were always smothered in pig parts, we weren't getting them from anywhere else. I can't remember the last time I ate vegetables before her.

The best part about Miss Angie was her hours. As long as I kept food in her fridge, I could get a hot meal at any time of the day. It could be three or four a.m. after the after-hours and all I had to do was knock. She'd hop up and start frying, baking, and microwaving shit. I'd kick back and light a blunt. By time I was finished smoking, I'd have a five-star hood meal waiting.

I kept the drugs a few blocks away on Port Street. We called it 2020—that wasn't the address, it was just a name I gave it. The house used to belong to Nick's grandma but it has been boarded up for years. Rats ran in, out, and then back in again just like they did when she lived there. I had a junkie rig the power and we were on. The kitchen cabinets were full of vials and cooking supplies. I put a TV with some bootleg cable in there so we could watch games when we capped up, and his grandma's old furniture was good enough for us to use so we used it.

CASHLAND AND MADEIRA

Money rained from the clouds and spilled in every direction. You'd be hard pressed not to see a loudmouth fiend in bent-up Air Force 1's hollering about "Rockafella, Rockafella, Rockafella! Rockfella—the best rock in the city and it's six dollars a pill! You heard it right baby, six dollars a pill!"

Yeah, I dropped those pretty purple-tops, sixes of Rockafella, and set the hood on fire. Everyone affiliated with me was making money, even the non-workers. I couldn't whip the batches up fast enough. Cases of gel-cap vials stacked in the kitchen, and if we weren't trapping, we were packaging. It got so crazy that I didn't have to promote my rocks. The crackheads became walking commercials. My smokers used to sing about it all day and we never ran cheesy gimmicks like buy one, get one free—my cook game went up three levels to the point where the drugs were so good they sold themselves.

Other hoods started calling their crack Rockafella just to get some of our overflow. Hurk wanted to kill over dope names. He'd fill his clips up to the tip and chant the same thing over and over: "These niggas dead, man, I'm icing these niggas, man, for real, man."

I'd pat his back with a wad of cash like, "Calm down, boy, we gettin' money, our shit fold. They money jingle!" And I'd repeat that over and over again, making it into a song until he was forced to laugh too. And why wouldn't he? He never saw that kind of money, or thought he would see that type of money. I remember when his ass showed because he had holes in jeans and boxers. I tried to control Hurk to the best of my ability, but I couldn't baby-sit him 24/7. One day a fiend stopped Hurk on the block, complaining about how Rockafella was the shit, and now it's some shit.

He showed Hurk the counterfeit rocks that were passed off as Rockafella. Hurk whipped out his gun and demanded to be taken to the salesperson, who ended up being a kid named Skinny from Belnord with four huge gold teeth that poked out of the front of his mouth, like his jaws were a hot nightclub and they were on the guest list waiting to get in. The fiend directed Hurk to Skinny and Hurk directed his pistol to Skinny's mouth. He used the butt of his gun to slap all of his gold teeth out. I heard he held him down by his neck and beat the side of his head with the gun until pus squirted out. Skinny came to me a day or so later with a mouth full of chipped-up loose teeth, dangling gold fronts, a lopsided swollen head, and an apology.

And then there was the deaf crack fiends that screamed on us, and the angry white junkies who demanded a substantial refund because they considered themselves to be loyal Rockafella users, and a bunch of other sales ranting and complaining about being burned.

"Hurk, we can't fuck everybody up!" I said.

"Yo! Nigga, we worked too hard for this! We just ain't going let no bitch nigga run off with our dope name! Fuck outta here!" Hurk yelled at me, waving his pistol like a baton, spit diving away from his mouth and running down his face in every direction. I laughed.

"Hurk, we really didn't work that hard for it. I inherited this shit, remember? And then put you on. Remember?" I responded with a shrug.

I guess he bought into the illusion of our new wealth. He thought we truly earned the money that basically fell into our lap. We weren't really anything but some hood trust-fund babies.

"For the tenth time, Hurk, you can't beef and get money. The two don't mix!"

I didn't care if another crew ate of my innovation because I was moving what I had. Plus, I wasn't going to beef. I told myself every day that I wasn't going to be that petty guy who had to suck up every dollar. I'd never murder over money. I didn't even care if you were making money, as long as I was getting mine. As long as I could stack a few hundred grand without shooting anyone while I figured my life out, met some girls, and had some fun. And all of the above was happening.

Girls came by to see us as much as the junkies did. Tall ones, short ones, pretty and chocolate and thick and stick-bony and good and bad, light skinned, brown skinned, and from the county and from York Road and Loch Raven and Essex and Whitlock and Chapel and Douglass and Up-Top and Down Bottom. They were employed, jobless, beautiful, smart, silly, funny looking, ran credit card scams; urban models, rappers, church members, club queens, and hustlers. I loved them all. They were all so different but really the same. They all wanted the same thing. They wanted to be affiliated with us. They wanted to say that they were fucking with the hottest niggas, who stand up on dirt bikes in the middle of traffic, ignore authority, and risk their lives every day.

The niggas who tote pistols, never ask for change, own the nightclubs. Them niggas was us. The niggas with clout. We were the niggas who probably wouldn't live to see twenty, and if we did, then our names will be all wrapped around 250-page federal indictments and we'd probably spend the remainder in a federal prison. They'd come see us on visiting day with Gucci handbags, babies on their hips, and spend the rest of their lives saying, "My man locked but he was the shit when he ran these streets."

Jail was the bottom of my concern list, primarily because I had cash—the kind of cash that would allow you to beat a charge or two. The amount caught me off guard because it came so quick. Turning dope into dollars wasn't easy, but it was way easier than I thought. I put in so many hours that I really didn't have time to spend it. So many hours that my days ran together—Tuesday through Thursday felt the same, really only the first stuck out.

I didn't feel like going into the safe every day so I had a Hefty bag of cash in my padlocked closet and it was filling. Shit looked like one of those beanbag chairs—except it was stuffed with Jacksons. Loads of cash carry a delicious stink. My whole room smelled like composition book paper and pocket funk. Eventually the money started burning right through the door. Its stench seeped into my thoughts and nested. It consumed me. I looked at it over and over again. I couldn't stop stacking it and then reorganizing my stacks. It needed to be spent.

It begged me to spend it.

And why not? I was really comfortable. Selling crack felt legal.

But I knew it wasn't legal so I started buying good karma before I spoiled myself. Looking out for the kids in the neighborhood felt better than new clothes and sneakers. I liked to rent a couple of those big white family vans from Enterprise and fill them up with young people from the neighborhood. "Don't be like me; never sell dope" was the speech I always kicked our days off with. From there I'd take them miniature golfing and go-cart riding on Pulaski Highway. I gave some of the kids money to golf while the others raced me multiple laps around the track, and why not? I was eighteen, so I was kind of a kid too. From there we'd go to McDonald's, then Friendly's for ice cream, and then I'd give them all a twenty before dropping them off and returning the van.

I'm not crazy. I knew my brother wouldn't want me to be doing the drug thing, but he'd love my Robin Hood days. Plus, you can't treat every kid in the neighborhood to burgers and amusement parks with a nine-to-five—it's impossible.

IKE GUY

Troy parked his new Nissan Maxima by the curb and jumped out on me, his eyes brighter than the car. "Check my wheels, Dee! She clean, only sixty thousand miles on that thing!"

Troy's my homie from Down Da Hill. He never a sold a drug in his life and didn't even think about it. Selling cane wasn't him and he knew it. Troy was like my only friend who didn't sell drugs. We are the same age and similar in most ways, into the same things—even making money. Troy kept a legal job, had a t-shirt line that faded, and tried all of those stupid direct marketing pyramid schemes. His latest gig is at a dialysis unit.

"Oh, yeah, she nice, bro, I see you doin' you, I gotta test drive her," I said, crushing weed and placing it evenly into a cracked cigarillo.

Selling crack was not legal, my homie Troy told me every day. He kept saying we should buy a store or get a car lot but I didn't know anything about that and neither did he.

"One time yeroooooo! One time yerooooooo!" shouted Dog Boy from across the middle of the street. Young Block had enough time to slide into Angie's house. Sirens erupted and flooded from both ways. Ike Guy, with some narcs and their pistols, crowded us like, "Get down! Get down!" Ike Guy was a real piece of shit.

He was this dickhead cop who hated black people, Mexicans, all minorities in general, and probably even white people with tans.

Troy, I, and the rest of us had lain on the concrete, facedown. Some plainclothes cops scanned the corner, looking for the ground stash. Grandmas who lived on the block stared at us out of their windows in shame, shaking their heads. And even though we broke their hearts by selling crack, I'm sure they still felt bad about the police dehumanizing us. Block walked out of Angie's, scooped a bag of pills from the downspout, and slid right past us.

"You a ugly little fucking nigger!" Ike yelled to Dog Boy, massaging his boot on his temple.

"You are ugly, right? Tell me how ugly you are!" Ike walked around Dog Boy's body and kicked him between his ribs until "Ugggggggggggggg" came out.

Dog Boy tried to keep a stone face—his lips trembled, he held his tears back by trying to keep his eyes wide open. I kept my eye on Ike's partner, Jones. He was black and let Ike say *nigger*. What a pussy and a disgrace to blacks, even more than us, I thought. I hated him just as much as I hated Ike, if not more.

"Booker, throw him in the car. I saw him make a sale!" Ike yelled, referring to Li'l Bo.

Block made it to the backstreet and smoothly bent the corner. Gone. Fire should've sparked out of his Nikes the way he jetted down the alley. Block's a housing project acrobat—jumping over gates, cars, people, hang-dropping from windows, sliding under cars, and he's the best at climbing trees, fences, walls, you name it and he can scale it. "That skinny kid is running, he must have it!" yelled a plainclothes cop, pointing to the alley.

"Fuck! Let's move out!" yelled Ike. "Let's move out!" The squad cars pulled off and we all hopped up and brushed the dirt off.

*   *   *

Cops like to come through Madeira Street and shake shit up like snow globes, but they never really locked us up. Well, I was never booked. Normally they just wanted a gun, because we weren't really making any noise. Sure, the lines were long and traffic was steady; however, our spot was new and getting caught with thirty pieces of crack, which warrants a kingpin charge, wasn't a big deal for us.

Guns were "get out of jail free" cards. Give the arresting officer a gun, and you walk away free with no questions asked. It didn't even have to be a nice gun—most of the weapons we had were old and rusty Civil War–looking pistols that probably didn't work. Some had jammed chambers and broken hinges and others were clipless and missing screws. The nice cops would even let you keep your drugs. Ike wasn't one of those guys.

Ike was a terrorist. A gun wasn't enough. He'd take a gun, and then he'd take your drugs and go for your self-respect. Ike liked pressing his pistol to your dome as he made you lie on the ground while he dug in your pockets, clearing them of everything including cash, cigs, your lighter, chewing gum, matches, and even the lint. You better not be broke—being broke when he was thirsty for money could warrant a beating. Fifty percent of my scars came from Ike, which is funny because he can't even throw hands. I saw him get whipped three or four times by young boys half his size. Ike was five-foot-ten with a thin nose. His complexion is pale milk. He's medium built but male-titty sloppy and weak—weak physically and mentally. Weak physically because I never saw him on the winning side of a brawl or tussle; he always ended up on the bottom. Weak mentally, because he was more of a crook than us. And yeah, I get it, I get it, we were the bad guys, and he was responsible for chasing us, but I never felt like that was his main concern. He didn't give a fuck about the community he worked in.

You'd think hustlers like us hurt the community but at least we shared money and employed people, while Ike cursed out old ladies as he cracked the shit out of their grandsons. We legitimately had a great product and sold it to customers who wanted it. He wanted a piece of our proceeds, if not all of it. Every time they rushed I understood that. But I'll never understand the way he treated non-dealers. Every black kid in east Baltimore is not a drug dealer. Most of those cops knew who hustled and who didn't. Ike Guy would just see a crowd, pull his Chevy up on the curb, and club whoever, like he really didn't know the members of the community he patrolled.

My younger cousin Tatter Man, who never broke a law in his life, came through the block to get some money from me for his prom one night. I hit him with the cash and we walked down to the Chinese spot to get some shrimp fried rice and gravy. Tatter walked out the door in time for one of Guy's sweeps.

"What the—is that your dinner?" yelled Guy to a confused Tatter.

"Yeah, I got some rice, what?"

"Boy, you being smart!" Guy responded as he knocked Tatter's food to the ground. I watched from the window as Guy used his boot to smash the rice into the concrete.

There was no negotiating or deal cutting with him, so I committed to his rules. I set money aside for buying guns. We had a box of pistols, but not for war—they were all for the cops. Dickhead cops like Ike existed all over the city; he was one of a thousand. I just wanted to sell rocks, and not worrying about jail made it easy. As soon as the cops cleared, it was business as usual. The line reforms and the money starts coming in.

"See, man, that's why you gotta get off this corner! I know you got money, man, so just get a job. I'm not gonna keep coming to see if it means laying on the ground, boy! I work too hard for my money!" Troy laughed while reaching out for a handshake. I walked him over to his new ride and took a look inside.

"You doing good for yourself, man! Keep up the great work," I told him.

"Yo, I can plug you with a job whenever you want, bro, just let me know!" said Troy as he pulled off. I waved a peace sign and shouted, "Naw, bro, you work too hard!"

Sad thing is that I wasn't joking. He worked about sixty hours a week at that place and could probably barely afford his used Nissan. My runner probably made more than him. At times Troy told me he couldn't survive without all of that overtime. What if they took that away?

THE BEAST

The streets have a way of making goofy, fun-loving kids beasts—bloodthirsty money grubbers who focus only on capital and power. I didn't realize that I was a beast until a dope fiend named Rolo hit our stash. He stole like a hundred dollars' worth of drugs and received an ass-whipping that could cost $3,500 in medical bills easy.

I cracked his head like a coconut with a broomstick and emptied his pockets. Nick kicked his head in until it leaked. Rolo would've died if Li'l Bo hadn't stopped it—and Li'l Bo only stopped it because Rolo was his uncle. We thought we had to show junkies and other crews that we were animals—not the kind you pet and love, but the ones that would rip your head off and piss down your throat. Every segment of our diverse clientele took notice.

Some of our junkies were in wheelchairs and some limped in floppy shoes and others had two straight legs. Some junkies worked at Hopkins and drove nice cars, some worked for the block on 100 percent heroin salaries—100 percent heroin diets too; well maybe 98 percent, because junkies loved honey-glazed, jelly-stuffed, and powdered doughnuts. I saw them swallow those sweet things whole without chewing. Our junkies looked like the mother from *Fresh Prince* or Bill Cosby and they all yelled funny curse words like Samuel Jackson. They always danced even when they weren't trying. They were white, whiter than Klan sheets—whiter than the drugs we sold them. They were black or Mexican with big belt buckles and pointy boots. Some junkies were deaf and screeched out their orders in sounds and hand gestures. We didn't care about disabilities; if you had money, we'd serve you.

If you were a mom, or pregnant, or a teen, we'd serve you.

We were beast. Being beast made us free—slaves to money but still free. Being a beast felt great. It's sport. My uncles were players, my brother was a starter, but I'm the MVP. And why shouldn't I be? I was there, I was in the center. I was an orchestrator. As a kid I stayed away—even though this stuff always went on right in front of me, I remained clear. Most of us try to stay clear until we grew up and became a part of it. Your mother can't protect you from it; mine tried but I still was presented with a chance to make my own choice like everybody else. Bodies always fell and fat mothers, fat grandmothers, and fatter aunts always hit the scene screaming and yelling, "WHYYY!" up to God. God never really answers them back but if God were to answer, the response would probably be something like, "Cuz that's just how it is!"

The beast only allowed us to feel the murders of the people we knew—the ones we had real attachments to—meaning fuck the guy who got shot up the street; if we didn't know him, it didn't matter to us. The minute you try to connect with the pain of the community in general will be the same minute that the beast will chew you up, and spit you out too. The beast allows you to be content with the idea of being buried before your mom and grandma.

This is east Baltimore and everybody will get a chance to be in a fucked-up situation—you'll have to shoot, or be shot, or be arrested, or beat down, or robbed, or kidnapped or tortured or murdered.

The beast will guarantee that.

*   *   *

I got used to it and it became my life. I would throw on the latest just to post up and watch my team. We were staples in this community. We polluted the block. We were responsible for the traffic, the tragedies, and the pain. We didn't live there, but we did. Day in and day out, decked in whatever anybody wanted—threads, kicks, haircuts, technology, and everything else. We introduced the hood to videophones, platinum chains, and diamond-covered teeth. Adolescents ran past us, pointing at our sneakers, clocking our cars, dreaming of being us, asking their moms can they be like us. They idolized us just like we idolized Gee and the dealers that hailed before. The dealers that introduced us to beepers, gold ropes, Cazals, box fades, 740 Beamers, and silk tank tops.

I had been selling drugs for about a mouth now and I kinda had this game figured out. I bought my workers thin platinum Cuban-link necklaces and the fiends knew that shit. If a junkie rolled up on someone selling six-dollar yellow-tops of Rockafella, Phat Cat, White Diamond, or whatever I called my product that day, they knew to look for that necklace.

I also never ran a dirty strip. I hated trash, so I kept Ashland and Madeira trashless. I used to tell people that it was so clean you could eat off of the ground. I paid junkies to pick up the trash and they worked in shifts just like the dudes that hustled under me. The residents appreciated that. I didn't hold them hostage and they didn't give me a hard time. I called them sir and ma'am, my workers never disrespected them, and I even kicked a little cash to the church programs, youth sports teams, and whatever else Angie recommended.

I was the boss, so I rarely touched crack or guns or money at all anymore.

Really, I only touched basketballs, *Robb Reports*, big butt Trina, marijuana sticks, Keisha from Chapel Hill Projects, fried chicken, sweet tea, and girls my age named Tonya or Tarsha.

Other than a few run-ins with the law, Ashland and Madeira was almost drama free.

COMING TO AMERICA

Hurk and Nick were sick of me riding around in their cars. They complained about how I adjusted their seats because I liked to sit upright—being all dipped back made me dizzy—and they hated how I took out their Project Pat and Juvenile CDs and threw in my favorite albums—*Illmatic* and *Reasonable Doubt*. Hurk was always like, "New York rap over, nigga! Get on this south shit!" Nick especially hated when I didn't turn his radio down before cutting the car off.

"Nigga, cut the beat off before you cut the car off, my speakers gonna blow!" he'd yell and I'd just say, okay, my bad, next time. Plus, I left change and ashes and girl paraphernalia all over the place. They were neat freaks when it came to their cars. Every CD had to be organized, new vanilla trees dangling off the rearview with a spare tree in the glove box. And I also never parked close enough to the curb for them and didn't refill their gas tanks. Who carries a parking ruler around to measure how many inches the tire sits away from the curb? Who likes filling up gas tanks? Those cars were attached to their identities, they meant everything to them—but to me they were just cars.

"Where the keys, Nick!" I asked.

"Seriously, dug, you need your own shit! I'm gonna get wit' this chick," he barked before leaving our crib one night. And then that became his response every time I needed the wheel. Hurk would just disappear. I got it. It was time for me to buy a car.

When I told Hurk and Nick that I was about to bust out with some new shit, they harassed me every day like, "What you want, a Benz? A beamer? What you gonna get, man?"

"Chill. *Coming to America!*" I'd say. "*Coming to America!*"

They'd look at me like I was crazy. And maybe I was a little off. Our Percocet habits were growing, so we were all always semi-fucked-up most of the time. I say semi because we stayed alert enough to conduct business. I used to break my 30's in half and give the rest away—my own special way of telling myself that I didn't have a problem.

Nick was worried about me upstaging his Lexus. That was his baby. He washed it more than he washed himself.

"Yo, you gonna wash the paint off that car, man!" was what me and dope-fiend Fred used to tell him.

"Dee, what you driving? Nuffin? Ah okay! And Fred, you never had a car and you prolly never will never get one because MVA don't let junkies drive!" is how Nick responded. Nick really OD'd on that car. He placed a Lexus car cover with a huge Lexus logo over it when it rained, or when the sun shined too hard, or just because. The leather was perfect, not a crease or crack, and he hit the dash with Armor All every day. Nineteen-inch Lexanis were his wheels. They shined like lit diamonds when the sun hit them. Hurk didn't go as far as Nick but he loved his ride too, and I felt him. Even though I bought Nick's and put Hurk in the position to get his.

The AutoGuide advertised deals and sales on all types of cars in the Baltimore area. Everything was in there from new Jags to rare Acuras, but what did I want? I knew I didn't want something that was too flashy; however, I did need a car that said I was the man, because I was.

Dog Boy helped me out: "A truck will be dumb hard. Get that, bruh! What twenty-twos on dat hoe!"

"You see, Dog Boy, I'm not a truck guy. I need something that's like *Coming to America*, you feel me?" I said, circling some Audis and handing him the book.

"*Coming to America*? Like Eddie? Fuck that mean, dug?"

Coming to America to me basically meant a smooth and clean showstopper. When Eddie Murphy's father the king hopped out, you knew he was somebody special. He had a sense of regal power that screamed, "Bow down! Don't fuck with me! I run shit." That's what I wanted.

"Dee, you know what! You need some kinda Benz then."

I flirted with that idea. That's what everybody expected, so I made the call.

"Seth, what's good!"

"Dee, what do you need? I just got some amazing stuff in."

"Cool, I'm coming up."

VIRGIN GANGSTERS

Me, Dog Boy, and his homie Long Tooth piled up in a hack. A hack is an unofficial cab in Baltimore that will take you anywhere for five or ten dollars. I normally pay twenty dollars. This one was a Chevy with beige cushion busting out of the seats, a lint-covered interior, and it smelled like Brut and Black Ice.

Long Tooth was Dog Boy's new worker. Dog Boy quickly advanced to my little lieutenant. I gave him the last of my heroin, which was about 250 grams, and he set up a little shop on Ellwood and Monument. It was a test that he passed it with flying colors. Dog Boy ran the shit out of his shop. He recruited Long Tooth to help him out. They'd met at Hickey reform school back when Dog Boy sat a year on some petty drug charges. Long Tooth was being held for a murder, but he beat it. I don't know if he did it or not, but I took an instant liking to him.

"I'm really going ride in my first Benz today, Yo. Dis so crazy," Long Tooth whispered to Dog Boy from the backseat. He really looked up to me, I could tell. But they don't really give direct compliments where I'm from; you have to maintain a sense of arrogance. Long Tooth was as skinny as Dog Boy but tall. Not as tall as me, but he towered for his age. His teeth were piled up like New York traffic, one covering the next with no space in between. One long tooth hung from the top of his mouth and almost scraped his bottom row when he talked—hence the name "Long Tooth." He was really into guns. Long Tooth kept a gun mag rolled up in his back pocket and a .50 cal in his dip.

"What color you want, big brova!" Dog Boy yelled to me.

"I don't know. Roll the weed up, LT. And Dog Boy, make sure that money right."

Hacks let you smoke weed if you tip a little extra. Some even hit the blunt. This driver didn't want to smoke. He was an old church nigga from around the way. We never knew his name, so we called him Unk. (Basically any old-head or dope-fiend or old-head-dope-fiend from Baltimore goes by or will be called Unk at least once in his life.) This Unk gives people rides to and from church on Sundays and hacks in front of the Stop Shop Save Market on Monument Street during the week. We always saw him around.

"Bitches gonna go crazy over dis car, Dee!" Dog Boy laughed. He organized eight stacks of my money on his lap while he talked. Each stack was five thousand dollars in evenly folded twenties.

"They gone go crazy anyway! Speaking of that, where y'all girls at?"

I saw Long Tooth stare out the window from the side-view mirror.

"I still be fuckin' Kearia, dat's my baby, ah nigga try get her I'ma fry his ass!" said Dog Boy, reaching for the blunt. I passed it to him. The driver laughed. "Damn, you only got one girl?" I asked. "All that fuckin' money ya ugly ass have! And you only got one girl?"

"She the only one that's trying to let me fuck! I mean some sales sucked me good but I only got that one body."

I looked at Long Tooth. "Damn Yo, and you ain't getting no pussy either?"

"On some real shit, Yo, I'm a virgin. I ain't get none yet but I came close like twice."

We all busted out laughing. Unk spun his Kangol to the side and told Long Tooth "That first piece of ass gonna feel good to ya, boy. When I got my first piece of pussy, I came quicker than a Monday! Whooooo! I tell you I came quicker than the cops in a white neighborhood! Mannnn, that twat was sweet!"

"Hold up, man! Hold up!" I said. "You mean to tell me that you shot somebody, been to jail, and never had no pussy? Damn!"

I told them to relax, they were now on my to-do list right after buying a car and securing a drug connect. I was going to establish their sex lives. Unk pulled up in front Seth's. I hit him with sixty dollars.

"Y'all be good and don't spend too much time chasin' that kitty kat! Haaaa," said Unk as we exited the car.

MY FIRST BENZ

Hello, welcome to the Foreign Auto Exchange, how can I help you guys?" she said. I paused for a second. We all did. She had a latte tone with dark curls. The only thing more perfect than her smile were her lips—or maybe her skin.

"Seth, I'm looking for Seth," I replied, all awkward and goofy.

"Dee? He's waiting for you, let me go back and get him."

Her teeth were flawless. She could've modeled for Colgate or sold Crest ads. Seth walked out. "Dee! Come on back." I tried not to glance at her as we walked past. Seth's office was clean and organized. The last time I came he had contracts scattered, but now I could actually see the color of his desk. Pictures of his family and exotic cars lined the walls. I also noticed that those broken-down Legends and Vigors were gone.

"Damn, Seth, you really fixing this place up. What's up with the girl?"

"Ahh, Asia, she's great for business. Guys see her ass and buy cars they can't afford! You see her ass? Look at her ass before you buy a car!"

"Naw, not yet." I laughed. "What you got for me, though?"

Seth walked us around his lot. Dog Boy and Long Tooth were two steps behind me. I wanted them to see this side of the game. Not me fucking up money, but how these white people who didn't

88

really care about us easily kissed black ass for money. If we were broke, he'd ignore us, but money made us his equal. Money made him embrace Bip, embrace me and Nick and now Long Tooth and Dog Boy.

A couple of Caddy trucks, some Porsches, and a few Lexuses were parked around the lot. They were showroom clean and I was impressed. Seth told me that the MVA was cracking down on dealerships like his, so he was slowly switching up his business. He wasn't slanging raggedly luxury cars on their last leg anymore and was being more careful with titling. I told him that my situation was the same. I'm buying a car. I don't have a real job, and I'll probably never get one, and he can put it in anyone's name he needed to as long as I had the title.

Dog Boy found a Beamer. "Dee, the five series wet, bro! This it right here!" Seth quickly said he could cut a smooth deal on that car but I wasn't with it. The 5 series was nice but I knew too many chicks with them. I considered 5 series, A4's, X5's and Lexus ES's and really anything in that grade or price range to be girl cars— middle-aged-stay-at-home-bake-cookies-for-the-soccer-game mom cars—baby-mother-mobiles. I needed some king shit.

"Seth, you ain't got nothing for me!" I said, patting him on his back. "Maybe I should go to CarMax and build some credit or some shit."

"No, no, no, tell me what you want and I'll bring it back from the auction tomorrow. We'll detail it and I'll certify it!"

I told him that I wanted a Benz, an S500. Long Tooth and Dog Boy's eyes stretched across their faces. I then told Seth that I wanted it to be as new as possible. I agreed to pay cash and let him know that I wasn't paying that brand tax that commercial dealers try to put on people. Fuck that, I knew the prices.

"Gimme some of the money and I'll have it delivered." I had Dog Boy give Seth $20K and told him he'd get the rest after he delivered the car. Seth gave us a Camry to hold while he found my dream car. I asked if we could keep the Camry too and he asked for $10K.

"I only got eight on me, man. Wassup?"

"Do we always have to do this? Nine and a half."

"$8,250 or I ain't buying shit!"

He took it and I agreed to do the paperwork another day. I knew I needed another car. I didn't want to drive my big shit every day. Nick hit me up on my way back down to Madeira Street. He was all excited, saying that he had big news. I didn't catch him that night but the next day he said that we had a new connect. A dude named Rex from west Baltimore who was fresh out of the feds and back to slanging bricks. Nick already set the buy meeting up, which would take place in few days.

"This nigga gonna look out for us, man!" Nick said as we all sat out on Angie's steps. Madeira Street was changing. We used to be the only guys out here, but it was hot now, loud music banging from multiple houses and forty-plus people hanging. They were kids in Polo and jumbo-sized hoodies, smoking and drinking, all passing the bottles to the right and the blunts to the left. Kids with no curfews were everywhere like they never had parents. The people that flooded this block never had anywhere to go but here. Most of them didn't hustle—they just wanted clout. Being out there around us instantly gave them clout.

The sun faded and the crowd thickened. Young Block took that Camry out to grab us some re-released Barkley sneakers and I was stuck hearing Nick go on and on about this connect. A dark Benz rode past us, circled the block, and then stopped. A pretty woman peeked out. "Dee, come over here!" My niggas embarrassed me with "Ohhhhhhhhh," on top of "Who dat? Who dat?"

I squinted. It was Asia. "That's my whip, man, y'all hop off my dick!" I yelled, running to the car. Nick shouted something like, "No, this nigga didn't!" I made Asia pull off before my friends could get a look.

"Oh, my God! You hang out there with those crazy people. I thought you were nice! Do you want to drive your car?"

"I am nice and you can drive. Are we going back to the office to settle up now? Or you wanna chill with me for a little while?" I asked.

"Chill with you? I don't even know you. Plus you aren't really my type," she said, making the left onto Route 40. I asked her how could she know that I'm not her type if she doesn't know me. That whole statement sounded stupid. I told her to run me past my crib so I could get the money to pay for the cars. We pulled up to my house and I ran inside and grabbed an empty Crown Royal bag. I stuffed it with about forty thousand dollars in hundreds. I hopped back in the car, and we headed to the dealership. She told me that it was nothing personal but she didn't date African American men.

"Aren't you black? I don't get it."

She then told me that she was from Ethiopia. She was a Towson student and quickly learned that African American men weren't *men*. They were scum. They had a monopoly on ignorance, AIDS, and were not good at anything but being ignorant and getting AIDS. She wanted no part of that. No part of the flash, no part of stupid rap music, no part of African American culture in general. She dated a white guy named Ralph. We pulled up at Seth's. I told her that some of us are different and every race has good and bad people. Then I wished her luck with her studies and completed my transaction.

The old me would've tried to explain African Americans to her. I would've called her general and tried to persuade her to accept us and our flaws—and be proud if she was receptive to the message. If she wasn't receptive, I would've called her a stupid bitch. But the new me didn't give a fuck. I had money. Enough to buy her if I really wanted her. She was one of a million girls and my new car was more interesting, anyway.

An hour later, after I finished the paperwork, I jumped in the driver's seat, pumped that big-ass plate-sized gas pedal and sped off, gunning down Route 40—my Benz was equipped with navigation, heated seats, all types of lights and buttons with buttons for the buttons. I didn't have any music so I cranked 92Q. Jay Z's "I Just Wanna Love U (Give it 2 Me)" was on! I opened the moon roof—"I'm hustla, baby! I just want you to know!"

REX RULES

Re-up time came around and Nick and I were off to cop from Rex for the first time.

Rex lived in the Northwood area of northeast Baltimore. His neighborhood was full of trees, grass, and driveways—shit we never really see. Some consider it a hood, probably because of the dense black population and Baltimore's rep in general, but that area was a dream to kids like us. I mean, most of the families around there went to college, hung up Christmas lights, and were probably homeowners. There would probably never be a boarded-up house around here.

When Rex opened the door, he was wearing full Muslim attire from head to ankle, that matched his black Nike boots.

"*As-salamu alaykum*, come in." His beard was long but it didn't fully connect. Small dark frames hugged his puffy face enough to make a set of creases on the side of his temples.

"*As-salamu alaykum* means hello and peace be upon to you. Every time you see your brother, you should bless him," said Rex. Some bottles of oils were scattered around his crib, and black artwork was everywhere, from African masks to those annoying paintings they sell at flea markets of the muscled black dude riding a lion and wearing a crown with his black queen in one hand and Mother Earth in the other. He also had books that matched his artwork on the table and chair; some were cracked open with bookmarks poking out. A jump rope was on the floor by some Perfect Pushup bars—the combination of which could be united to become a hood nigga's Bowflex.

Rex used to be a wild pretty boy who talked about nothing but banging his gun and getting his dick sucked; now he was calm and smelled like incense.

"Y'all young brothers ever think about converting to Islam?"

Conversations about religion make me bored. Rex went to jail for four years and now he's Minister Farrakhan? I didn't get it, but Nick loved it.

"Off my din now but I'm a get back on ahk."

Nick's a jail nigga too so he slips in and out of religion. He should identify as a Christ-slum—Christian when he's home and around his mom, Muslim when he's locked.

"With all due respect, fellas, I ain't trying to explore religion. I'm down to my last li'l bit of powder and I need you, man," I said.

Rex asked me to stand up, saying he wanted to get a good look me. He said I wasn't the kid he remembered. He remembered me chubby and happy—an innocent virgin on a dirt bike with clean Nikes and a mouth full of butter-crunch cookies. Love was in my eyes and my smile. Love was in my walk and followed me as I ran up and down Fayette Street. And now I was in the game—and cold like everybody else.

"You know, Dee, you could maintain that happiness you had as a kid and survive in this game if you built a relationship with Allah." I held in my laugh a little but some chuckles slipped out. I couldn't figure out why he didn't understand that I wasn't looking to be saved, and if I was, I probably wouldn't have a drug connect as my spiritual advisor.

"Let's rap about it later," I said with respect. Disagreeing could have turned into a ten-hour conversation on Muhammad's philosophies. I learned early not to have arguments about religion.

Rex said he'd hold me to it and asked how many ounces did we want. I laughed again and said, "A hundred and eight ounces of your finest cane."

He took his small glasses off and said, "Come again now, you really want three bricks?" I took the JanSport off of my back and unzipped it enough for him to see that it was stuffed with cash.

"Told you we was out here doing us, man." Nick said to Rex, slowly placing the cash on the table, preparing for it to be counted.

"Hold up, shorty, I can't cover that today, but I'll give you two for forty."

"That's steep, and we buying two, man." I used to look up to Rex but now I'm taller so he had to look up at me. He stroked his beard with his left hand while his right hand was tucked in his left armpit. "Okay, li'l Dee, gimme thirty-eight. That's a great price."

"Rex, bro, I'll get you thirty-five and you can sell us that other one as soon as you get it."

Rex agreed and went into his basement and came back with a leather ottoman. He sat it down in front of us and opened it. Some Folgers cans were inside. He pulled them out one by one until he reached the bricks. He tossed one to me and the other one to Nick.

I nicked the plastic rectangle with my house key and put a little on the edge of my mouth. My eyes twitched as it dissolved while my tongue furled and touched the back of my mouth. "This will do!" I said. We counted that money out, paid, and bounced.

Nick and I cruised down Ashland Avenue. I had spent a bunch of money in the last two days, and I was glad to be putting work out.

"Why you be dismissin' Allah and Jesus all the time?" asked Nick with a straight face. Most Baltimore people are the same when it comes to God. They do whatever they want and then use their part-time religion as a front to make them feel better when they mess up. It's like they don't feel bad when they commit a sin, but only when they get caught. Getting caught instantly brings the religion out.

I pulled over and looked at Nick. "Yo, I don't reject any God, I just don't know. Like God wants us to be happy, right? I'm never happy. Everybody is dying and if this God wants us so happy, then why is religion always about punishing yourself? Like no pork, no alcohol, only fucking one girl, and being nice to everybody! Man, fuck that! Heaven and hell is right here on earth and all of the hypocrite drug dealers and evangelizers like Rex are the ones who were confused!"

DINNER AT ANGIE'S

I clipped my half blunt and pulled my Camry up on Madeira Street. My young guns were out hollering, "Rockafella! Yeah, dat Rockafella out!" Alicia Keys was on. She made playing the piano look so cool—like what if I played the piano in Jordans with gold teeth: no one would expect that. They'd think I was coming to stick the place up and then I'd just bust out with a selection from Bach and shock everybody.

A white man who looked liked he stepped out of a JCPenney ad walked into Angie's place and walked out about ten minutes later, shaking his head. I saw that Angie was crying. I decided I'd fix her later.

Block was running the shift change, and the new stuff from Rex was cranking. I stayed in the car and watched the same customers come back and back again. I wondered why they never just bought three or four. The same person would come back to our block and buy one on six or seven different occasions. I'll literally see that they had enough for three or four and they'd be like, "Just one. I'm only doin' one more." Maybe it was just an illusion of self-control. Maybe I did the same with Perks, popping four half-pills in two hours, acting like that shit don't add up.

Troy texted, *Bro you down the way?* I told him yeah and come through. Troy had been getting at me heavy over the last few days about one of his patients and how I needed to meet him. He kept calling him an old head gangster and said the three of us could do business. I wasn't really sure at what point Troy started taking a personal interest in my business, but I bet that Benz had something to do with it. I don't think he thought I'd be rolling like that; no one really knew what I was holding. Troy was like family so I was willing to entertain any idea he had, but that car was a magnet for dick riders: everybody wanted to kick it, borrow it, be around it or in it. I got so many waves when I rode down the street, I felt like the president. I never knew owning something like that could be so exhausting.

Troy rolled up around twenty minutes later. I was in the mix of about forty-plus loudmouth, Niked-up teens and early twenty-somethings in a huge circle. Crackhead Lenny and his wife, Loraine, were in the center wearing big red boxing gloves, getting ready to beat the shit out of each other like gladiators.

"Left hook, Loraine! Left hook, Loraine!" some kids yelled as she belted Lenny into a three-point stance. Loraine stepped back, Ali-style, and danced a little while waiting for Lenny to gather himself. The crowd thickened, and Ike Guy and his cop friends came by to watch and made side bets like, "Lenny, you're goin' to jail if I lose another fifty on you!" I never gambled on junkie fights, but I'd always watch.

"Dat nigga done! Dat nigga done!" was the usual chant when Lenny couldn't get back up. I saw Loraine beat Lenny's ass a thousand times.

One time Lenny had a *Rocky* moment: he lunged forward with an overhand right that connected perfectly with Loraine's chin. She swallowed the blow like a small pill and finished him off with two to the gut and a firm hook that stood him straight up before laying him out like school clothes. She then picked him up as always and gently placed him on a stoop like an infant before claiming her prize, twenty dollars' worth of crack and some high-fives from us. They'd go back to their junkie-love right after they received the drugs. Junkie love is the realest. We all saw it before, two inseparable fiends who are always together 24/7 on a mission, always fussing but never breaking up, always connected at the hip, always sharing that last blast. Lenny and Loraine were committed to each other but married to the drug. The combination created a love that most people will never see. I was never fooled by the fights because their love was real.

The guys on the block I hustled with lived for these fights, or dope fiend races, or drinking contests. Basically they loved a Junkie Olympics made up of anything they could bet on, and most of these events ended the same: the losers trading money for cheap shots from the winners, as we all reported back to our posts. The hustlers would go back to hustling, the police would go back to policing, and the junkies would go back to chasing.

"Let's rap, Dee!" said Troy as he walked up.

I gave him a five and said, "Let me handle something real quick; walk me over Angie's, dug." Angie and her fat wet face was sitting on her stoop. Her muumuu was wrinkled and she rocked back and forth.

"Angie, what's wrong baby?" I said, patting her back.

"So much is going on, you hungry? Lemme make you a dinner."

Miss Angie is the definition of power. Women like her are the most powerful people in the black community. Single mother or not—diabetes or high blood pressure or whatever ailment, black women like her remain the most consistent. They keep food on the table, they keep the lights on, they keep a roof, and still have money to spare for the church, the lottery, their kids and their kids' kids. A lot of fathers bail. Women like Angie don't.

"Yo, Troy, you hungry?"

Troy said always. We sat in the kitchen while Angie started dicing up onions.

Miss Angie went on to tell us how she raised generations of children in this house, how her husband bought it for them when he came home from the war, how she buried him and her oldest son in that house—her fat hands were magic, she cut and whipped and seasoned; the smells intoxicated us, my stomach clenched—she could walk to church, the market, and the hospital from that house, she cooked meals for the entire neighborhood here. She lost the house after her husband died but the buyer leased it to her, and now he just tripled the rent on her and said she had to pay it or leave.

"I can't afford to stay! Who gonna cook for y'all when I'm gone?" She placed chicken in the oven and started prepping sides. Tears fell and she just kept moving. Troy looked at his feet and shook his head.

"Damn, Miss Angie. They on that gentrification bullshit around here. He just trying to tax, what he want?"

"He said twelve hundred a month!"

Troy yelled, "Damn." I laughed. I couldn't stop. They looked at me like I was crazy and I kept laughing.

"Stay right here!" I said, running out the front door. I grabbed my bag out of the car, walked back into the kitchen and pulled out fifteen thousand dollars. Angie's jaw hit her house slippers. Troy's face was identical.

"Pick your mouth up, Miss Angie!" I said, still laughing. "You do so much for us, fifteen racks ain't shit. Pay it for a year and keep the change." She leaped across the kitchen like Jordan and squeezed me dizzy. I lost my wind and had to pry her off of me. Troy kept saying, "That's such as blessing, Yo."

Now I smelled like her house—grease, mothballs, Icy Hot, and all—but I didn't mind. I was happy that she was happy. Troy and I inhaled her plates and walked back out front. Hurk was across the street shooting dice with Fat Tay, I hadn't seen him in a few days.

"Dee, you the shit man! For real, man, you a one of a kind." Troy said, looking at me all crazy like I was a prophet or something.

"Whateva, man, anybody in my position would've did that, she a nice woman."

"Yo, your position is exactly what I wanted to rap to you about. I'm ready to do what you do. I'm ready to sell dope, man. I want to drive that car and help people like Angie and I got a way in. This old head at my job saying he need some kids like me to move some stuff. His son got locked. He likes my personality and I wanna do this but I can't without you. Can you stop past my job and meet him?"

"Yo on some real shit, lemme think on it. I'll holla at him if you want and if it's not a good look, I'll set you up with us. Just make sure you really wanna do this."

Troy thanked me a thousand times. "I love you, man," was the last thing I heard before he pulled off.

"Hurk, what's up?" I yelled across the street.

"I don't know, man, you tell me?" he responded as he took two steps back, and rattled the dice in his left hand, then jumped forward and spun them across the concrete. Ohhhhhhhs erupted from the crowd.

I grabbed the clip I had earlier and re-sparked it.

KNOCK 'EM DOWNS

The dope was gone and, Dog Boy and Long Tooth had moved a block over to Jefferson Street, to build a little crack spot down there. Crack spots were much easier to build than dope strips. Crack spots are like pop-up shops but established dope strips are like department stores. I headed there to give Dog Boy an eighth of cane.

I took Block with me over to Dog Boy's grandma's. Dog Boy was about to cook for the first time, so I wanted to be there to coach him through it. Usually me or Nick did it for him, but he was ready to learn and I wanted to make sure he didn't fuck the batch up. Block was older than Dog Boy but didn't want his own strip; he was good working with me on Madeira. Dog Boy's grandma Faye was like family. Our whole hood greeted her like, "Hey, Aunt Faye." She really loved me, all of us, really; we could go into her fridge and everything. I walked right in without knocking.

"Y'all li'l niggas got money now, y'all can't be leaving the door open!" I said.

Long Tooth nodded in agreement. He got up and started checking the rest of the doors and windows. A huge pistol rested against the small of his back.

Diabetes chopped Faye's foot off a year or so ago so she couldn't get around and clean like she used to. I made Dog Boy have her house cleaned by fiends when he and his teenage friends had her crib smelling like armpits and ass. Her chairs were wrapped in plastic and she had a big bowl of fake fruit on the countertop, and a zillion fruit magnets on the fridge; so many that you couldn't even see the door. I wish she had the same obsession with real fruit, because I never saw an edible piece in that crib.

Like Angie, Faye had a white Jesus on the wall too. It's like they gave that picture to every forty-plus black woman in my hood— probably in every hood. You couldn't find a crib without Martin, JFK, and that Kenny Rogers–looking Jesus.

"Big brova, I know how to do it, I just need you watch me! Feel me?" Dog Boy asked. I pulled a huge cup of Belvedere and removed my shirt. I never met a person who cooked crack with a shirt on. "Let's do this," I told him, walking into the kitchen. Long Tooth took notes.

"Yo, your li'l ugly ass can get closer, you need to learn this too!" Block told Long Tooth, pushing his shoulder. Long Tooth inched forward. Dog Boy talked his way through the cook: "Add dis, add dat, whip dis, sprinkle dat..." Dog Boy whipped up a perfect looking batch. I thought he may have cut it with a little too much Arm & Hammer, but his rocks still looked really, really good.

"Yeah, I see you cheffin', Dog Boy! Good shit! But I'm catch y'all guys later, I gotta handle something!" yelled Young Block as he approached the door. He was always handling something or somebody. Dog Boy slapped the rocks on the table. The three of us sat in a circle and proceeded to bang up the work. Dog Boy used aqua blue tops and called his crack Big Dick and Li'l Dick. Big Dick was the dimes and Li'l Dick was the nicks.

"Li'l brova, you callin' your drugs dick and you get no pussy, you wanna tell me something? Dog Boy, are you eating pickle?"

"Fuck you, Yo." Dog Boy laughed. "I fucked my girl earlier!"

We capped up every spec. I was proud of my little guys.

"Yo, y'all want some girls?"

"Sure," they said. Long Tooth looked nervous.

"Yo, you walk around with big-ass guns and sell a bunch of drugs! Relax, it's time for you to start fucking too," said Dog Boy as I popped a half Perk and washed it with the Belvey. Alcohol makes Perks feel 200 percent better. The three of us loaded up in my Benz. I had some girls that I could call who would be more than willing to date them if I asked, but I wanted them to score that night, so I took them to see the Knock 'Em Down Girls.

Knock 'Em Down Girls were a group of teenage prostitutes who lived in a house on Erdman Avenue. I don't know the history behind the Knock 'Em Down Girls or who originally coined the name; however, I knew that you could fuck for forty dollars and fuck someone really attractive for ninety dollars. This round would be on me, and I was treating them to nineties.

We pulled up out front. The upstairs lights were off but the living room was bright. I saw shadows walking back and forth so I knew they were home.

"Yo, if y'all don't wanna do this, it's cool. I'll take y'all home," I told them. I didn't want to fuck anyone in there, but I wanted to treat them.

"Man, I'ma suck a bone out one of dem pussies!" said Dog Boy, dipped back in the passenger seat.

"Man, you crazy!" I said.

I took a blunt out of my glove box and we hopped out. Three minutes of banging on the front door and big Doula opened up. Doula's a house of a woman. Taller than me and wider than the three of us put together. Her arms were tree stumps, her back was an Escalade: she probably had to enter the door sideways.

"Dee muthafuckin' Nice! My li'l nigga!" she said. "You finally tryin' get ya dick wet wat us, huh?"

"Naw, not me, baby, tonight is about my young boys." She rubbed her hands and invited us in. The house was clean and plain with no pictures; it looked like a model apartment or a Value City Furniture showroom.

"Mickey! Key Key! Come on!" Doula yelled. In a split second two beautiful young women ran down; they looked twenty-something. The one on the left was fucked up on pills or drink—still prettier than any of the women I've seen work in that house before, even though she was high as gas prices.

"Dog Boy, you should take the one on the left!" I recommended and he agreed. I didn't want Long Tooth's first time to be with someone who wasn't completely present.

"Long Tooth, wassup? You wanna do this? You got a rubber?"

"Chill, Dee," the girl said, "I got 'em." She grabbed him by his hand and led him upstairs. "Ah baby, be gentle, it's his first time!" I laughed. Long Tooth cut his eye at me in embarrassment. I waved him off. Dog Boy and his lady followed.

I flopped on the couch. "Doula, wanna hit this blunt?" She walked my way and extended her arm. I passed her the jay and she took a long pull—a pull long enough to take a half inch off of the blunt. A pull only someone with jaws as big as hers could take.

"Damn, girl, slow down!"

A stampede of coughs and chokes poured out of her. I should've told her that I cut the blunt with hash. That shit hit like Tyson in '89.

"Hakkkkkkkk! Haaaaak! This some good shit, boy!" she moaned. Doula sat next me. We shared the blunt while I waited for my boys. Some other customers started rolling up. They had to wait outside until a girl was free.

"How's business, big lady?" I asked.

"We gettin' money like you, luv! Bout ta take my girls down black bike week in South Carolina, that's six hundred dollars a dick down there!"

Long Tooth ran down the steps with big eyes that wrapped his face. "Dee, you ready?"

"Are you?" I asked.

He wanted to go back in one more time. Doula and I laughed.

"Don't kill her!" she said. "We got other customers waiting!"

STEEL SHARPENS STEEL

Forget a blood connection, Nick and Hurk are my brothers. Fuck that, they are an extension of myself. Talk shit about Nick or Hurk and I'll slap your face before you get the words out. If you're bigger than me I'll crack a Rémy bottle across the side of your dome. I remember when Nick played with toys and Hurk used to name the roaches in his crib so I can never front on them.

"Yo, you need to rap to Hurk, man, ASAP!" Nick yelled through the gate three times straight. His pudgy fingers gripped the fence. We were down Bocek Park. Baltimore greats that turned pro like Sam Cassell and Muggsy Bogues used to play here back in the day, but no one fixed the court up. The pavement was cracked and uneven, and sometimes I had to kick the shit out of junkies so they would get up and let kids shoot around. The only new items in the park were the nets that my friends and I hung when we had hood versus hood games. We normally played for five hundred a head against surrounding blocks and other crews. Some girls will grill, blunts get passed, bottles get drained, and these events are normally peaceful. We had a hood game coming up in a few weeks so I'd been sneaking and trying to get a little practice in here and there. I was trying to get my jump shot working against some middle schoolers. Same form Bip taught me back in the day—bend

107

your knees, flick your wrist, slap a rotating arc on it, and leave your form up as you watch the ball fall through the bottom of the net every time.

I wanted to be a pro ball player way back when I was a kid but I grew out of that quickly. People don't understand how talented professional athletes are. Being the best in your town or city or state isn't enough. You have to rank among the top in the world. I wasn't even the best in my house plus stupid dirt bike tricks and Pop Warner football mangled my left leg, making me walk like a seventy-year-old. So yeah, my hoop dreams deflated a long time ago.

"We gone rap later, I'ma see him at Moe's," I told Nick.

Later came quick on that day. I beat Hurk down to Moe's. "Dee, how are you, my friend!" said a guy working the door. I gave him a pound, five dollars, and asked him to watch the car. They know me in Moe's, because I've probably eaten there at least once a week since I was an infant. Moe's is known for Maryland crab cakes. Maryland crabs are different from any other place in the world. We have a zillion big-ass blue crabs popping up in the Chesapeake Bay every day so seafood restaurants in Maryland can't be skimpy on the crabmeat. Popular spots like Moe's use huge pieces of jumbo lump and almost no filler. They were also known for a number different seafood dishes as well. I tried them all—except the ones with thick chunky mayonnaise-textured imperial sauce. There's nothing more disgusting than imperial sauce. I'll eat a woman's ass, but I won't eat imperial sauce.

I grabbed a table near the bar. The server came out with a double shot of Belvedere chilled. Hurk and his new bling strolled in. He was a walking jewelry store wearing too many chains to count. He also had some heavy bracelets that sparkled.

"Damn, homie, you about to shoot a rap video?" I asked, waving the bartender. I needed another shot.

"Yo, we playing in the hood game, right? A thousand dollars a head against them Perkins niggas. I'm bustin' they ass, you hear me!" Hurk replied, loud enough for our whole side of town to hear. The waiter bought him some Belvedere too. I ordered a crab cake.

"Yo, you ain't getting no food?" I asked Hurk. He ate imperial sauce and ass.

"Naw, man, I ain't eatin'. I'm just telling you that I'm done with Madeira Street. Like if you buying from Rex, I got money and I can buy from Rex too. Feel me? No hard feelings, though, just this three-way split is dumb. I'm in this shit to win it. Feel me?"

"I hear you, but I don't feel you. We make each other better, we got each other's back, man," I said, trying to make eye contact, but he looked away.

"Yeah, I know, I know steel sharpens steel and all that dumb shit, but I'ma do me. And you do you."

Hurk dropped some cash and slid. I sat a minute, had three or four more drinks. Stayed a while longer. I started this to make money with my friends, I thought, knowing I had just lost another brother.

SWEET SONI

Soni and I met at Jazzy Summer Nights, this outdoor jazz festival Baltimore had every first Thursday during the spring and summer months. You could catch anyone of any class or any color dancing, buying handmade jewelry, or like me—getting Len-Bias-on-draft-night fucked up. I'd throw some Perks in me, put on a new shirt, and then bang my liver with half a fifth of Belvedere before heading down with Dog Boy playing copilot. Sometimes Nick came down too.

I felt like being out. The split with Hurk had been fucking with me. I really wanted to go and didn't mind going alone, but some bodies had dropped recently and Dog Boy wasn't letting me roll anywhere solo since the shootout.

We hit the festival an hour or two after it started. Dog Boy had been drugging harder than me—popping dark green PlayStation epills like Altoids, but I was Mormon sober that night. The Advil bottle that I'd stuffed with Perks in my glove box was empty, and we hadn't stopped for drinks.

"Dee, no bottle? You ain't cop no bottle? Shit, Yo," said Dog Boy, dying of thirst.

I reached into the backseat and grabbed the half bottle of Deer Park. "Here, drink this, dummy, we'll get wet when we get down there."

"Warda," he replied with a coiled face.

We hopped out of the car and I tried to hand Dog Boy some cash because we normally split up. He pulled a tennis ball–shaped bundle of twenties out of his sock, placed it in his sweatpants, and said, "I'm good, baby, put your li'l money away."

Me and Dog Boy combed the crowd—him looking for vodka, me people watching, and us both looking for girls. We bumped into Tank, an old friend from Perkins housing projects. He and Dog Boy instantly dived into conversation about New Balance's best shoe or some other topic that I didn't care about so I wandered. I walked past the main stage once or twice and peeked in at each and every concession stand. Everyone in the crowd wore grins; problem-free looking women in flowing dresses twirled while their soulful dudes in linen pants and open-toe sandals danced by their sides. I wondered what they all did for a living. Did they hustle? Was I the only one who cared about fluctuating coke prices? Could they tell that I sold drugs? I noticed Dog Boy from afar and easily would have been able to tell he hustled if I didn't know him. He looked eleven years old, an eighty-pound teenager with Queen Elizabeth's diamonds wrapped around his wrist, gleaming from here to wherever. Dog Boy, like me, would mix diamonds with loose Nike sweat suits or Louis Vuitton Damier print belts with Timbs. Only drug dealers mix and match fine European fabrics with apparel you can find in USA Boutique and the Locker Room.

Dog Boy was still rapping to Tank. He positioned himself like he was firing an AR-15 while Tank gyrated with his eyes rolled back in his head—as if he was taking imaginary shots from Dog Boy's imaginary gun—shit hood kids like us do when we've eaten one too many paint chips. Watching them act like that made me laugh while making the more reserved blacks uncomfortable. They always looked down on us and they always will.

Fifteen minutes of strolling aimlessly through the festival and I had yet to get a number or a drink. I passed a few women who had been past my crib before—cute baby-faced brown girls infatuated with niggas that sling dope, baby-mothers of retired gangstas, county girls eager for a project tour, and women old enough to be my mother. Some would speak with that neck twist I loved while others showed me their middle fingers, but either way was cool—I valued my experiences with them.

I grabbed a strawberry piña colada frozen umbrella drink from a stand not too far from the main stage and saw a new face—a woman that I've never seen before. She was standing alone, draped in Afrocentric fabrics and had about fifty bracelets on her right arm and none on the left. It was weird but kind of fly. I walked a little closer.

Her Scotch-colored skin was flawless. I bet she never took a drink, tried a drug, told a lie, or had a problem—ever. I was never the guy who cared about skin color, especially inside of my own race. I'm addicted to all black women and twisted every shade from Pepsi-colored to flake-colored and light-skinned women who were bright enough to gain Klan acceptance. She was probably one of those back-to-Africa chicks, I thought, so I couldn't approach her the same way I would roll up on these hoodrats. I'm literate, I'm kind of smart, I'm clean, I thought—fuck it, I'm going in.

"Hey," I said as I stood in front of her.

"Hi, ummm," she replied, looking over my shoulder. "You're blocking the show. I'm kinda into it."

"Oh, I'm so sorry," I said, quickly moving to her left. Normally

I would've had a clever response but I froze, and being extra nice was my natural instinct.

"You wanna drink?" I asked, still looking for an in.

"I don't drink, but thanks. Wait. Are you serious?"

"What?" I replied as I saw her looking at my necklace. I was wearing a diamond-cut Cuban link, with a Jesus-head charm hanging in the center. The crown of thorns had about three hundred diamonds and the eyes were rose-colored rubies.

"Why are you wearing so many diamonds? Do you know where they come from?" It was hard for me to focus on what she was saying with those cosmic eyes staring straight through me.

"It was a gift from my older brother. Too much?" I asked.

She went on to tell me about Sierra Leone and conflict diamonds. She said that children lost dreams and limbs so that people like me and rappers could be blinged out in gaudy, pointless jewelry. I listened to every word she said. I never saw a person so passionate about something that they could never profit from. Soni went on to tell me that she was a college student and planned on going into the Peace Corps after graduation.

I lied and said that I was going back to college in the fall. Then I quickly switched the topic to the impacts that Malcolm X and the Black Panther Party had on African American culture, pride, and black awareness, which basically means I told her everything I know, except my drug knowledge. She nodded like her head was on a string, while adding a feminist perspective. I was probably the only young dude in the city that looked like I represented the street but could hold a conversation about awareness and Black Nationalism.

We exchanged numbers. I didn't want to be too forward. She sparked a sense of negritude in me that I hadn't felt since Bip died.

I heard Dog Boy calling me as we parted ways. I turned around to get another glimpse of her before leaving the festival and caught her looking back too—our eyes met again.

"Yo, who that big head bitch, y'all related?" said Dog Boy.

"Naw, she my new friend," I replied while looking down at her number in my phone and making sure it was saved into my contacts—I was notorious for not saving numbers.

"Okay, okay, let's hit Scrawberries, tho. Dat's where da real hoes at anyway. Fuck these bitches down here." Strawberries 5000 was a nightclub on Route 40. The loosest of the loose women went there looking for guys like us—brash dealers who would aimlessly throw money at them. We were regular in there. We spent thousands when we came through. In exchange we never paid cover charges, could get kids like Dog Boy in, and were exempt from frisking.

"Fuck is a *scraw*-berry? Strawberries, my nigga. Strawberries."

LITTLE DEBBIES AND AUTOMATIC WEAPONS

The smell of fried hair and fuck clouded the air when I woke up around eight a.m. the next day. I rolled over and cracked the window to get the used, condemned smell out. Twenty missed calls flashed across the front of my Nextel—some from Gee, some from my aunt, and then some from a bunch of random people—but no Soni. A small, wasted, healthy ass attached to about three hundred dollars' worth of fake hair slept at the foot of my bed, butt naked and hazel colored with socks on. She snored like her lungs were broken. Her gums were dark, but her teeth had orange plaque caked near the crown, like she ate too many Cheetos. We had all definitely been on that Cheetos and vodka diet the night before. About another $450 worth of fake hair attached to an even bigger, rounder dimply ass was stretched across the floor next to vomit and an opened box of Magnums—another night after Strawberries.

I snatched the bottle of Belvedere of off my dresser, took two big gulps, and braced myself as it warmed my chest. I thought I would let the women sleep a little before I kicked them out. That was, if Dog Boy and Nick's argument about religion didn't wake them up. They had those dumb fights every morning.

"Fuck you, Nick! I thank this nigga Jesus for crack sales, for my big dick, my bitches, in dezz automatic weapons a nigga-blessed wit, may I kill niggas who act dumb. Amen!" yelled Dog Boy, jumping from the kitchen to the living room and back.

"Y'all bitches shut up, these girls are asleep!" I yelled downstairs. One of the young ladies rolled over and said, "Who you callin a bitch? Your mother a bitch, I ain't no bitch." Then she rotated back into her snore.

"Naw, Dog Boy. Allah put you here. You gotta think, Yo, get on your din," replied Nick, not loud enough to outyell Dog Boy.

"Shut the FUCK UP!" I yelled, going back into my room, trying to return some of the phone calls. Dog Boy banged on my door and then went to the bathroom. Surprisingly, the sound didn't wake the girls up. I sat back and thought about Hurk and why he was acting like he didn't need us. Like we haven't been like brothers since we were kids. Like I didn't cut the money up evenly, like he ever saw this much money in his whole life. Hurk was important in keeping my operation going.

But do I really want to keep this operation going?

My mind had the happy faces from the jazz festival on repeat. They sang, smiled, danced, wore printed bow ties, and called each other *brotha*. We call each other muthafucker, dummy, bitch, and pussy as if they were our first names. No bow ties and funnel cake over here—just pain, Little Debbies, and automatic weapons.

I picked up the Tech 9 lying next to the half-eaten oatmeal cream pie on my dresser. Resting the gun on my chest like a newborn blessed me with ease. I've never shot a person and I probably never will, but having this just made me feel good. My thoughts of making the transition to the other side were really scary—IRS-coming-to-audit-me scary.

Those people who looked happy easily fit into my definition of broke. They couldn't drive what we drove, go where we went, or fuck who we fucked—two nameless women in comas occupying my space. But what would I do, work at FedEx? I couldn't wear a FedEx short set out here in these streets. Those women don't fuck Comcast installation men or UPS workers—who would probably give them gifts and attention, unlike me, who only offered new ideas on pleasuring me. They were only here because of what I do in the street. I couldn't differentiate between them or the ones that stayed over the previous night, and I liked it. I liked the money and, more important, I liked looking out for Dog Boy, Angie, Nick, and the rest of my people who couldn't take care of themselves. They needed me.

"Dog Boy, you still in the bathroom?" I said, opening the door.

"Yeah, Yo, get the fuck out!" he yelled, sitting on the toilet Indian style—sucking his thumb like a toddler. The shit dripping out of his body smelled so bad that you could hear it. I muzzled the lower half of my face with my right hand and grabbed his bag of blue-dolphin-epills off the sink with the left.

"Yo, no drugs and shit when we doing business," I said, slamming the door.

"What you mean business, Yo?"

"Hurk really not rockin' wit us no more so you gonna meet the connect."

His eyes lit up like Christmas Eve. "So I'm going? No problem, I ain't pop yet," replied Dog Boy. I kicked the girls out, giving them his pills as a parting gift, and called Rex to tell him that Dog Boy would be coming up for the first time. Rex lived in the city but stopped keeping his drugs in Baltimore. He kept the work with one of his Muslim brothers in the Eastern Shore of Maryland and we had to ride out there to get it—that's like a three-hour ride from Baltimore. We stopped at the McDonald's on Fayette Street, copped a fish for me and nuggets for Dog Boy, and hit the road. Dog Boy leaned his chair back, ate gray meat nuggets and shuffled through the pages of an outdated *Don Diva* magazine. He didn't read the stories but loved to look at the images of the drug dealers who kind of looked like older incarcerated versions of us—the jewelry, the cars, the women, the weapons—the game.

I didn't even listen to soul music like that but Lauryn Hill's *Miseducation* was on repeat—probably because her skin tone and hair style were like Soni's. I normally listened to Raekwon's purple tape before drug deals, but Hill's voice gave me a tingle, took me to a special place. "Nothing Even Matters" sounded like the conversation I had with Soni the previous day. I wondered if she liked me too as we floated up the beltway.

"Yo, get the fuck up!" I yelled to Dog Boy, beating his chair like a drum. Rex's Eastern Shore spot was a storybook house, country as shit with a white gate and a detached mailbox. He greeted us in the front lawn.

"*Salaam*. Is this the kid Dog Boy you told me about?"

"Yeah, this is my little bro. He's the youngest dude on the street putting in real work," I replied. Dog Boy's eyes expanded when they shook hands. His meeting Rex was equivalent to a teenage ball player meeting Michael Jordan. Rex was a drug connect, "The Plug," what every kid who plays this game where we come from wants to be. Rex's spot was super clean to be a stash house. It had some Pier 1 looking furniture offset by designer appliances. He had prepared dinner for us—fried plantains, some type of fish, and rice. We laughed when Dog Boy said, "Wat dey is fried bananas, Yo."

The three of us exchanged ideas on sports, the dope game, and life after hustling over the meal—a conversation that Dog Boy could never fully comprehend but he still remained cool. He didn't brag or even talk that much, called Rex sir, and even made us laugh. I was proud of him.

"You guys are welcome to stay, it's getting late," Rex said as we finished up.

"We got customers waitin', man, gotta roll, but thanks!" I said, loading the bricks into the passenger door of the car. The side panel snapped off and they fit perfectly, right around the speakers. Dog Boy dozed before we hit the beltway so I cut the music down and let the little soldier rest in peace. I flipped my phone open to check my missed calls—Fat Tay (3), Nick (2), some random blocked calls, and Soni (1). I dialed her number . . .

"Hello."

"Hey, Soni, wassup?" I said, trying to sound laid-back and cool even though my heart pumped out of my tank top.

"This isn't Soni, she's brushing her teeth."

Who brushes their teeth at nine thirty p.m., and why is this person answering her phone, I thought. "Can you tell her to give me a ring please?" The anonymous girl who turned out to be her friend Meka agreed, and we hung up.

I didn't want to throw money at Soni, but Bip used to always say that "everybody had a price," or that "everything cost everything all of the time," so if I couldn't hook her with my words, I'll find a way to pay to play.

Dog Boy was a vegetable; a car wreck couldn't wake him. I reached over and buckled his safety belt.

Ring ring ring . . .

"Yo," I said.

She laughed and replied, "This isn't Yo, it's Soni."

We dived right into a conversation that I tried to control. She knew about hood movies and hip-hop but could also speak about their negative and positive influences on different levels. Soni got all of my jokes and ended up being greater than I already thought she was. Her pops used to hustle but ended up as a junkie. His bad decisions shaped her into a politically conscious woman who really wanted to help others.

"We should hang out tomorrow," I said.

"Why? You think I like you?"

"Well, normally every woman likes me, unless they're gay. Are you a lesbian?"

She laughed again and said, "I don't know" before agreeing to let me take her out the next day. Dog Boy woke up around the time we were driving through downtown. I was just hanging up with Soni.

"Luva boy, we clubbin' tonight? I got a bitch that'll put hickeys on ya dick too. She bad," said Dog Boy as he made his body into a capital T shape and yawned.

"Naw, li'l bro. You a boss now, we gotta go bust this down."

"Right, we got business, I ain't dumb for real. Bitches can wait," he replied, curling back up into a lowercase *o* in the passenger seat, resuming his hibernation. Dog Boy slept the rest of the way, until I pulled up in front of the crib. Troy was out front waiting.

"Yo, I gotta play that's gonna make us a lot of money! Man, what's up!" Troy said running up on my car as I parked. I rolled the window down. "Yo, come in the crib."

Nick was on the couch asleep and I didn't want to wake him—but I'm sure the smell of the cooked crack would.

"Dog Boy, you wanna whip your shit up?"

"Yez zir!" he replied.

I laid my supplies neatly across the countertop and quickly fried up seven ounces of butter. People had really cheapened the Rock-afella name by trying to imitate us, so I decided to call this new stuff "Church."

"I'm proud of you, Dog Boy, but you gotta know that this shit is temporary. I've been thinking a li'l bit," I said as I razor-bladed a new box of vials open and Dog Boy carried the new crack rocks over to the kitchen table.

"Yo, you always talk like I'm post to do wat you do. Dee, I ont go to school. I ain't no book nigga. I'm doin' wat I'm post to be doin'," he replied while struggling to get a hard rock into the thin cylinder.

"Dog Boy, hold it sideways and slice these small rocks into thirds, they'll fall right into place. Yo, I'm not trying to son you but I hope you know that this shit don't last."

I realized that I couldn't sit around and tell Dog Boy that he shouldn't hustle while feeding him money and drugs—I had to show him. Being a criminal is part of our makeup and someone had to break the cycle. I wasn't really sure how, but I was thinking about it.

"I agree with Dee," Troy said. "I'm not a street guy by far, but I want to do one move with Dee, and then I'll never touch a drug again. We need to start a company."

"Exactly, you not street nigga, Troy, so why you in the convo? Shut the fuck up, I won't listen to niggas in nurse pants," said Dog Boy.

I laughed.

"Chill, man, he my family like you, that's why!" I said. I had to get up and carefully show Dog Boy how to put together the work.

121

There's no way he should want a career in this while only being able to cap up ten vials to my hundred.

"Yo Dee, lemme holler at you outside real quick."

I followed Troy to his car. He popped the trunk. A pile of scrubs that stunk of formaldehyde stared back at us. Troy looked at me and nodded with a slick grin. He pushed the scrubs to the side and showed me half a brick of heroin.

"Oh shit!" I covered the brick and slammed the trunk. "Where the fuck you get this! Boy, you can't just be riding around with all this."

The old head he had told me about fronted him the half and only wanted thirty thousand dollars back. He wanted me to help him knock it off.

"Dee, you'll love my old head man. I keep tellin' him how great you are. Please come by my job and meet him!"

He fronted my homie so I had to meet him. I agreed and we set the date for later that week.

DOG STORE

Li'l Dick! Big Dick out! Get that Dick Get that Dick!" a slumped-back fiend would yell in front of Kim's Convenience Store on Madison Street. Dog Boy and Long Tooth had copped that corner store so we started calling it the Dog Store. They didn't own it, but they paid rent to the owners—a Korean family who had been there for a year or two. Korean storeowners are temporary in the hood like us because they pop up, run their shop, and then switch the ownership over to their relatives. I think foreigners get special tax breaks or something. So they keep flipping owners when that tax bill comes.

Dog Boy kept anywhere from three hundred to five hundred pills for re-up in the store behind the chip rack on the floor. A Mac 10 was behind the poker machine and other weapons strategically lined the rest of the store. Long Tooth handled the bread and oversaw the smaller ground stash outside. Dog Boy liked to use different junkies as hitters day in and day out, preferably heroin addicts because he didn't have to worry about them stealing rocks.

"Yo, give dem hoes a blast in the mornin' and anova at night and they work hard as shit all day, twenty or thirty dollars' worth of dope and they work all day!"

I liked to watch those young boys work. They ran a tight ship and even though Dog Boy said he didn't want to be like me, his strip told a different story. Fuck, his clothes told a different story. Ravens fitted hat cocked to the side like mine, unlaced Air Jordans like mine, Evisu jeans like mine, spitting balls of gum five feet away into the trash can like me, standing like me, bouncing a tennis ball like me, walking with a limp like me, and his little ass didn't even limp—his legs were straight as shit!

His spot was doing well like mine too, and even though the Kims only let two grade school students in at a time, they allowed packs of crackheads to jam the store so a line wouldn't form out front and make the strip too hot. During a rush when his spot was flooded with fiends or when the cops hopped out on them, Dog Boy or Long Tooth would give large amounts of cash to the Kims. They'd hide it in the store with their own belongings because the cops never really fucked with them. The Kims weren't a special couple and it wasn't a race or ethnic thing. Drug shops were run out plenty of stores by owners with roots stretching from West Africa to East Asia and back. A lot of these businesses would fold without guys like us—to think we paid from four hundred to a thousand dollars a week just to operate and they really had no choice but to get paid because we were going to do it anyway. The other major benefit of the store was that wintertime flow. Baltimore winters are colder than Hitler's heart dipped in ice. Being stuck outside on the block meant chapped lips, ashy bleeding knuckles attached to numb hands, and aching-ass joints—the real grind. That's the part that rappers leave out of songs, that extra shit that's not mentioned in the job description.

DATE ANXIETY

Soni, we on tonight or what?" I asked. She paused. The phone was on speaker. Dog Boy covered his mouth, suffocating a laugh.

"You are so aggressive! Gosh, I have anxiety now!" Soni said. I heard her friends giggle in the background. "Yes, Dee, pick me up at eight, none of that two-hour late stuff!" We exchanged good-byes and clicked off.

"What the fuck is anxiety, like a rash?" asked Dog Boy. Long Tooth walked in yelling that Jay Z: "One million! Two million, three million, four! In eighteen months, eighty million more." Waving our cash, we joined in, like, "You now looking at one smart black boy!"

The idea of making it as big as Jay made us smile. He was our Bill Gates and his albums were literally the blueprint. Long Tooth—who started going by Young LT—was starting to get women and it showed. The grimy jeans and boots that used to be his armor had been replaced with new Polo shirts and bright Nikes. He kept a cut and baptized himself in Ralph Lauren Blue ten times a day.

"Yo, anxiety is what people get when they don't smoke weed, now roll up, LT!" I said.

"Got one rolled, here, hit this. You wanna pill too?"

I said yes to the weed and no to the pill. I didn't want to be too gone on our first date. "Maybe I'll grab one for later," I replied, taking the blunt from Long Tooth. Long Tooth's blunts were seamless—they looked like they've never been gutted and dumped. Shorty was the best at rolling, better than a Cuban kid in a cigar factory—he could even roll them perfectly while gloveless in a blizzard and posted on the block in fifty-below weather. Blueberry, the weed we had been smoking, had canceled my anxiety and I was ready to see Soni. We had talked on the phone a few times and each conversation was better and better. Effortlessly, she'd sucked up my attention and three hours flew by—to the point where the Nextel left burn marks on my ear and face.

I'm used to women saying *buy me a new weave, let's pop a bottle, I need a Loui bag, do my ass look fat, why bitches hate, cut the Hot Boyz on, you got some money, I hate my child father, I hate you, I miss you, I love you, don't fuck my friend, we getting money, I'll beat that bitch ass, I only wear 7 jeans, buy me a Gucci bag, buy me a dozen crabs, where the party at, where the party at, where the party at!*

Soni was all natural hair, fresh oils, the New Deal didn't do much for African Americans, seven gallons of water a day keeps my skin clear so it could work for you too, yoga, you do know the effects of chattel slavery still plague us, healthy eating is healthy living, the Trail of Tears was so sad, nature makes me happy, make sure you eat some vegetables, I'm a feeler because I always know how people feel, I love togetherness, you ever heard of Mumia, the Great Society, and on and on—she was like a walking encyclopedia without any physical flaws. Well, half of a walking encyclopedia because she never finished a lesson. Soni used to start off telling me about science or something in history and stop halfway through, like, "My memory is so bad, Dee, I'm taking gingko root extract so it's getting better!" I would always Google the rest, and I didn't care, I just loved hearing her voice and the way my name came out of her mouth, *Deeeeeee*. I learned so much in the short time we were talking, more than I learned in college. She was the first woman I craved in a nonphysical sense, which made me crave her in a physical sense even more.

I wanted our date to be right so I threw some new clothes on. I had bags of designer shit stacked to the ceiling that I had yet to touch. I decided to tone it down on the jewelry too because she thought I OD'd on platinum the last time I saw her. I kept it gangsta with a black tee, one thin Cuban with a Jesus piece, my stainless steel Submariner Rolex, some black Evisu jeans, and retro Charles Barkleys with the straps undone. Everything felt new, even me.

I looked at the mirror and Bip stared back, his features creeping in. I tied on a do rag—it was tight enough to make my waves pop, but loose enough to keep one of those dumbass lines from forming in the middle of my forehead. I planned on wearing it until I reached her block because dudes that wear do rags as a part of their outfits were corny. I sprayed six shots of Burberry cologne into the air and let it rain on me before padding my pocket with about $2,500. I knew I didn't need that much but I had to have it on me just in case; she needed to know that if she wanted something, I could get it. I looked at myself in the mirror one more time, plucked the boogies out of my nose and hit the window. "Kruger Man, get the wheels good, man! I be out in a minute." Kruger Man, the MVP of drug relapse, was cleaning my car. His face was long enough to fit a guy with a seven-foot-two frame, but he was five-foot-six so his chin reached past his chest. His body was riddled with pus-dripping cuts that never healed; it looked like his head was stuffed with cream cheese or custard. On Halloween we'd give him free drugs, a black hat, and clawed glove so he could scare the shit out of kids.

"All's clean, boss, and my God, she lookin' pretty! Almost pretty as me!" Kruger said, tossing me the key.

"Kruger, you ugly as two ugly motherfuckers but I love you, man!" I replied, giving him a handshake with a piece of crack balled up in a twenty-dollar bill.

Kruger cleaned the shit out of my car; it smelled better than a pair of new sneakers. The paint looked wet and the sun hit my wheels from three different angles, blinding anyone who tried to make eye contact. I thought about buying some aftermarket rims, but those factory joints looked perfect.

My favorite feature was the keyless entry. Not keyless as it hit a button and hop in, but keyless as in I didn't need a key. The car came with a small black card that fit in my wallet. As long as I had the card on me, I could get in and drive the car without the key. James Bond shit.

DINNER FOR REAL

Soni lived with her parents in Washington Hill, a little co-op near Chapel Hill Projects where most of the guys I played basketball with came from. Her block was clean, every house was refaced with fresh red bricks, the steps were marble, and there were zero parking spots—everyone in that community owned a car. I hit her phone. "Hey, I'm outside."

"Okay, I'll be right out!" she said. I whipped around her block and double-parked in front of her crib. Biggie's *Life After Death* cranked. I dug through my CDs looking for some soul music. She's a soulful woman; she didn't want to hear Biggie. I couldn't find anything and I saw her walking out, so I turned Biggie down to the lowest level.

She was wearing multicolored African pants and big colorful bangles.

"Wow! Nice car!" said Soni, hopping in. "Can I touch some buttons?" She was far more beautiful than I remembered, inside and out. Her energy took over my car.

"Yeah, you can touch some buttons, but where you wanna eat?"

"I don't know, you pick a place. This was your idea! Just make sure it's good. I'm small but I love food! Don't get it twisted!"

I ate corner-store chicken boxes or at Angie's all of the time; I didn't know anything about good restaurants. But I did remember that some of those dudes at Loyola used to talk about this place called Ruth's Chris Steak House near Little Italy. If they ate there, it was probably nice and Soni would like it, so that was my choice.

We breezed through east Baltimore, my huge car seats made us both look small. She turned up the radio. "Oh, you got Biggie Smalls on, Dee, okay!"

"Cut it out! You like Big?"

"Ten Crack Commandments" was on—she switched to "Notorious Thugs" and rapped every line word for word. I was really impressed. She caught me gazing, so I looked away. She giggled and spit every word from Biggie's to Krayzie Bone's verse. Who would've thought that this Badu-looking chick really loved Big— then I thought that Badu could probably spit Big's lines as well, which is why you can't judge a book. The song ended and she ran it back, and then again and again and again! I wasn't impressed anymore.

"Gah damn, Soni! Give Big a break!"

We laughed as I pulled up. I tossed the valet guy the key and we rolled in. Some of the patrons looked at us funny—the dealer and the healer. They probably thought she was dropping me off at a mug shot photo shoot on her way back to Africa.

"Welcome to Ruth's Chris, do you have a reservation?"

"Naw," I said, "but let me get a table of two, please, and nothing near a bathroom."

"I'm sorry, sir, we only seat people with reservations, unless you'd like to sit in the bar area."

"No, Dee, we can go to another place, I hate the smell of liquor!" Soni said, pulling my hand.

"Lemme talk to dude, give us five." Soni walked to the ladies' room. I told the dude that it was our first date and I couldn't fuck up. I pointed to an empty section and said, "Look, I'll give you a hundred fifty dollars if you can make this shit happen, right now."

We had great seats by the time she came back from the rest room.

"That bathroom was gross. What did you say to that guy to get these seats?"

"Nothing, I just told him that I was with the sweetest person in the world and asked him to look out."

She blushed while skimming the menu. "Okay, Dee, we should probably leave."

"What? What I say?"

"These prices are too high for that bathroom to look like that! I don't want you spending your money here! Can we please leave?"

She looked serious, so I said fuck it and we bounced. We hopped in the car and she said that the place made her nauseous and she didn't want to eat anymore but we could kick it. I was hungry, but I didn't give a shit—chilling with her was the prize. We pulled up in front of Federal Hill in downtown Baltimore and took a stroll. I found a bench that sat on top of the city; you could see everything from Canton to downtown and in between.

"So is dealing a part-time thing for you or will it be forever?"

I shrugged.

"I think I like you but I won't be with a dealer. Like what about the Dawson family? Some of you guys are the worst."

The Dawson family were all murdered on Eden Street. Their mom, Angela, kept calling the police because dudes was hustling in front of their crib. One of the guys from the crew heard she was the rat and threw a cocktail-bomb in her house, killing her, her husband, and her five children.

"I'd never do anything like that! You can't put me in that category! Those dudes were cowards!"

She told me how her dad's dealing and using had crushed their relationship. Drugs turned them from best friends to strangers. She said the car was nice and my clothes were nice and my smile was nice, but my job wasn't, and if I wanted to be a part of her, I needed to consider a change.

And dealing drugs and trash bags of cash didn't seem important while we had that conversation. I didn't think about drink, smoke, or pills the whole time I was around her. We just sat and talked until the sun came up.

Right there a future with Soni seemed possible, like something that could really happen.

WHAT THE FUCK IS
RENAL DIALYSIS

I walked in my crib around six a.m. and fell on the couch. Troy
beat on my door five minutes later.

"Yo, it's 6:05, cut the light off in the hallway when you leave
and twist that bottom lock."

"No, Dee, my old head. You gonna meet him today. Put
these on."

Troy tossed a set of scrubs at me.

"Are you fuckin' serious?"

I tossed them back. He caught them and shoved them in my
chest, saying that I needed them just in case a machine broke and
blood squirted all over the place.

"Blood? Why the fuck would blood squirt on me?" I asked.

"Because it's a renal dialysis unit!"

"What the fuck is renal dialysis!"

Troy explained it as being a place where they treated people
with kidney failure. I still didn't get it so I Wikipediaed it.

> In medicine, dialysis is a process for removing waste
> and excess water from the blood, and is used primar-
> ily as an artificial replacement for lost kidney function

in people with renal failure. Dialysis may be used for those with an acute disturbance in kidney function or progressive but chronically worsening kidney function therapy. Kidney injury is not usually reversible, and dialysis is regarded as a "holding measure" until a renal transplant can be performed, or sometimes as the only supportive measure in those for whom a transplant would be inappropriate.

"So you mean to tell me that it's like an oil change?"

"Exactly, and that shit come from high blood pressure, diabetes, and all that shit niggas get, so we gotta watch what we eat on some real shit, man. Niggas be getting they toes chopped off and everything!" Troy said. My quick burst of knowledge on kidney failure had woken him up. After I told him a little about his job, he dropped all of this *I'm an expert* shit on me. Troy couldn't have me knowing more about his job than him. I loved when my brothers flexed their smarts. I was mostly around people who only cared about a bunch of dumb stuff, dudes who were proud that they weren't smart.

"So what you do? They let you work with patients without being a college grad?"

Troy whipped into a parking spot, explaining how he's a reuse guy. A reuse guy basically takes the artificial kidneys (dialyzers) off of the patients' machines, cleans them on an even more flashy machine, and then stores them so that they can be used by the patient again during their next treatment. Each dialyzer got fifteen to twenty-five uses and the patients were treated three times a week.

"Damn, that's a good job, Troy; why you wanna sell smack?"

The clinic he worked at was nice from the outside. They had grass and a nice bench under a tree, plus there was a Subway sandwich store across the street. Girls with fat asses in tight nurse pants with elastic bottoms and Mickey Mouse print waved at Troy and walked in. I'd take this job over mine any day.

"Dee, I make eight seventy-five a hour as a grown man."

"Damn. Okay, well yeah I forgot, let's do this."

We walked through the double doors and around the back to the room where Troy processed the dialyzers. On the way, we passed a group of patients waiting in the lobby, mostly black and elderly. Troy's room was neat and clean like him.

"You wanna see what I do, Yo?"

"Sure," I said. Troy put on some latex gloves and opened a small fridge. He stuck his arm in and pulled out a bloody cylinder that was about twelve inches long.

"This is a dialyzer, Yo. Watch this!" He screwed a tube of water to the cap and turned the faucet on. A pool of blood spilled out, almost filling the sink.

"That's fucking gross, man!" I said, taking two big steps back. "How in the fuck is it so much blood in there?" I couldn't stop staring at the blood.

"These are full of special fibers that hold a large amount of fluid—think about those dumbass paper towel commercials where one towel soaks up a ocean. This the real shit!" he said, taking the caps off of the dialyzer and washing some meaty chucks of fat off of the tips. Then Troy hooked it up to a machine and hit start.

"Yo, I'ma go see if my old head here!"

Troy left me in his office alone. I played on my phone until he came back in around five minutes later.

"Yo, he here."

I followed Troy into the main section of the clinic where treatments occurred. Twenty patients reclined in huge beige chairs scattered all over the floor in a circle. Some laughed, some slept, some moaned. I walked past them and their identical set-ups—a tube of blood connected to their arms running into refrigerator-sized machines, flushing through the dialyzer and then circling back into their bodies.

"Why they arms so fat?" I asked. Troy said that normal veins are too small to undergo this type of treatment so surgeons stuff their arms with huge fake ones called fistulas.

"Troy, my boy!" said an old black guy tucked in the corner. His hat was Kangol and it draped over his small face. His skin was leather. He had two gold teeth, one on each incisor, and they shined brighter than the floors in the clinic. He was wearing a Rolex on the arm with the fistula.

Troy introduced us. "This is Dee, Mr. Pete, he helping out with that thing."

We exchanged hellos and Mr. Pete said, "Boy, have a seat!" Instantly, he started rambling. One of those ladies in the scrubs walked by. "Baby, you in for it, his crazy self gonna talk your head off." I didn't care; I liked listening. I was always a listener.

Pete said Troy was a stand-up guy. He said that people with open mouths had closed ears. He said the streets were as fucked up as his kidneys and lower back. He said crack fucked the game up but I'm on the tail end so I won't make any real money anyway. He asked if I had lead-paint poisoning and I told him no. He said I probably did and just didn't know it. "Everybody born in the eighties got lead!" He said fancy cars are dumb as the niggas who drive them. He said R & B is dead and rappers are crack babies. He asked what my mom did for a living. I couldn't answer because he instructed me to get him some ice in the same breath. The nurse said, "No! He knows he can't have ice!" He said come closer. I rolled forward and he said his kidneys don't work but she knows his dick does. I gave him a pound. He kept going and going. He didn't stop—race, class, religion, the streets, cops, sex, money. Three and half hours went by and I didn't even know it. I left the clinic and headed back to Troy's office as the nurse started to disconnect Mr. Pete from the machine.

"Yo, he loves you!" Troy said, loading the sink with a bunch of bloody dialyzers.

"How you figure that?" I said.

"Because he didn't ask you to leave, you'll see. He's gonna bless us. You should stop by sometime and see him too. He knows everything!"

I said I would.

THE GREEN HOUSE

I love Nick. He's a good brother, but—he was funky. He probably took as many showers as anybody else but he was still kind of funky. He's that pudgy guy with rubbing thighs who sweats in all of his new clothes. Once a week I had to tell him to keep drugs out of the house and that his girlfriends were loud. They all spit when they talk and stomp when they walk. Sometimes my hallway smelled like fat sex. I didn't want Soni to chill at this place, so I decided to grab a loft downtown. We had been kicking it for a while now spending all of our free time together and she even considered moving in with me. I had been wanting another place to live and the combination of my love and his funkiness gave me a reason to do something about it.

I had enough money to move wherever I wanted to, but the Green House was on some real boss shit—like if I ever got snatched by the feds, this would be the place I'd want them to show on the news. My brother used to date a Nigerian nurse who lived in the building. I had only been there two or three times, but I always knew I'd grab a spot in that building once I got my dough up.

And now my dough was up—really up—so I called the rental office and the lady invited me down. The building was located on Pratt Street, not too far from the Inner Harbor. A lot of doctors and healthcare providers in general lived in the building because the University of Maryland medical center was within walking distance. I greeted the rental agent with a handshake and asked to see her best unit. She said, "It's nineteen hundred dollars a month." I told her that I didn't ask for a price, I asked to see the best unit. She turned red and instructed me to follow.

The spot had wood floors, a billion-foot-high ceilings, and spiral stairs that led to the master bedroom, which was a loft overlooking your loft. Everything was open except the guest room.

"I'll take this!" I told her. I could already envision my furniture—white leather couches and a fish tank on some *Scarface* shit. I thought I'd make everyone take off their shoes once they stepped foot in my crib.

"If you like this place, we need to do a credit check, sir."

"No, we don't," I said. "I'll take it." I went to my car and came back with enough cash to pay the rent for a year. She gave me some papers to sign and I left with the key.

SMACK LESSONS FOR TROY

Troy hit my phone thirty times straight before I could answer; he left hour-long voice mails too, which were super annoying.

"Old head just blessed us with yeahhhhh, it's time to rock and roll, Dee! Old head asked when you was dropping by to say hi again too!" Troy said, breathing heavy through the receiver.

"We gotta rap about some other shit, Troy, let's link later. One." I hung up with Troy, realizing that I had to be very patient with him. He talks on phones as if nobody is listening and I'm not sure if they were listening or not, but I'd rather be safe than facing a trial date. He also needed to learn some simple how to's of this smack game.

1. How to drive. Troy drives like a nut, and you can't be like that with drugs in the car. Pull your seat all the way up, pop on the safety belt, cut the radio down, and go the speed limit. Never pull up next to cops, and don't make eye contact with them; don't even look at them.
2. How to act around girls. Basically shut the fuck up: girls will spend all of your money, get snatched up by the cops, snitch on you, and easily be accepted right back into society— fucking with the new dealer, the dude who took your spot.

3. How to treat your friends that don't hustle. Basically keep them away from this shit. I didn't want Troy to hustle but he paid attention to my every move and loved what I made. He was going to try this drug thing with or without me so at least I could keep him from doing something stupid.

4. How to stretch heroin. A little chemistry lesson was in order, that dope from old head was too good: fiends would die off of that, and the east/west dudes we hit with that first batch wasn't used to getting dope that good. They were stretching it too so we might as well get some of that money.

5. How to brand. Dope like cocaine, or Coke or Pepsi, McDonald's, Twinkies, Taco Bell, and everything else that will kill you needs to be branded right. It needs a strong, catchy name attached to a gimmick that will get the streets excited. Branding was my favorite part.

6. How to front work. He needed to know who he could trust when giving out drugs up front. I'm a big fan of the fifty rule, like you buy fifty grams and I'll front fifty grams—you fuck up once and I'd never do it again. And you always have to collect because if one person gets away without paying, nobody will pay you.

7. How to put some money up just in case he got booked. Public defenders will get you sixty years for one baggie. Troy needed real defense lawyers that charge like three or four hundred an hour, not some C student from a fourth-tier law school.

8. How to develop an exit strategy. I didn't have the answer to that one yet, but I was hoping we could exit together.

SHOOTOUTS

We were at the store. I pissed Hennessy in the alley, posted up by the open sign and spit some sunflower seed shells into a Nantucket bottle. LT was by the lamppost. He brushed his hair until his arms hurt while Dog Boy wore a big-ass money grin that wrapped around his whole head, and it was only right—his corner was bumping around 3K a day. I liked chilling on his corner more than my own. His little crew was funny as hell and full of innovation while all the dudes on my block except for Nick were jaded—always complaining about baby mothers, court dates, Sprint bills, being paid more, and long hours.

A Ford Taurus circled the block. The dude in the passenger seat poked his head out, "Dog Boy, we good, right?" Dog Boy waved him off.

"Who is that, Yo?" I asked.

"Nobody, Dee, just some loser-ass niggas," he said while a pack of kids rushed the door.

Mr. Kim walked out front with his broom and yelled, "Only two school kids at a time!"

Fall, my favorite part of the year, had arrived. Everything's orange and brown, the weather's perfect for a jacket or tee, and school is back. Little kids in their neat uniforms were everywhere, wearing clear book bags stuffed with dittos, compositions, and number two pencils. I liked giving them twenties and telling them to stay as far away from these streets as possible.

"Kim, they late for school, let them take what they want, I got it!"

Kim laughed and patted my back. "You big big rich man, thousand dollars for you!" The kids all grabbed Little Hug juices and big bags of Takis. Some more students and parents passed the store. Tyra, Dog Boy's sister, and his niece Muffin, a smaller version of Tyra, bent the corner, both screaming Dog Boy's name. Muffin spotted me. "Uncle Dee! Gimmie me ten dollars!" I reached in my sock to pull some cash out as that same Taurus whipped into the intersection in front of the store and opened fire.

Dog Boy knocked his sister on the ground and crawled toward the front door of the store. I laid Muffin under my arm and shielded her from the bullets. Some flew over our heads, and bounced of the wall. The door at the convenience store shattered as Dog Boy made it in.

"Get down, get down!" we yelled to some kids. LT stuck his arm out of the shattered glass and shot back at the Taurus. Then he covered Dog Boy as they both ran out of the store licking shots at the Taurus. The dude in the passenger seat shot back as they skidded off. LT caught one in the chest that went right through, I lost a little arm meat from being grazed, and a elementary school kid was on the ground shaking next to a big bag of spilled Takis.

"Get a fuckin' ambulance!"

Dog Boy panicked and tried to move the kid's body but I stopped him. As a kid my uncle Gee taught me not to move a body with a bullet in it because it could bounce around and hit an organ or something. An ambulance pulled up and then another along with some cops and a fire truck. LT and the kid were both rushed to Hopkins.

Cops had the same questions and got the same answer.

"We ain't see shit."

IN A TIME OF WAR

LT was laid up in Hopkins with a big-ass hole in his chest, and I didn't know if the little kid was going to make it or not. Dog Boy foamed at the mouth and strapped the band on his Tech 9 around his neck. "On my mova I'm killing every nigga wit' a Taurus, I swear for God!" His veins popped out of his skin when he spoke, his eyes were redder than the blood running down my arm.

"Go to your sister's and lay down, I'ma go holler at Nick and I'll be back down to get you!" I ordered.

He wiped away his own tears and headed out. "Damn, Dee, they hit you too!"

"Naw, a small graze, it just knocked a little meat off. Could've been from glass or the fall, no biggie. I'm good, lemme go round some soldiers up." Dog Boy hugged me and dipped.

I rode up to Madeira to holler at Nick face-to-face. I tried to keep a level head in the midst of all of this even though my chest burned with fear, but my mind spun in circles like a fan, flooding with thoughts, like we can't be reckless. But what if Long Tooth dies? Long Tooth isn't going to die but we had to do something. Who the fuck were those niggas? Did they know me? I'm not with this murder shit, I wish Bip was here. I banged a left on Madeira. My shop was closed. Tone's window was shut and it wasn't even noon yet. A few people scattered around my car as I parked.

"Kruger, where everybody at?"

"Ike Guy, boss! Fucking Ike! But Nick up in Angie's, can I get twenty dollars?"

"Damn, man, you see the blood on my arm?" I asked. "What the fuck is wrong with you!"

"Damn, Dee, sorry, you'll be okay. You gotta twenty? Can I wash the car later?"

Junkies always want something. He wouldn't care if I hopped out the car with my head in my hand, he'd still ask for something—a ten, a twenty, a bite of my sandwich, something. Kruger was no different than the cops in my eyes: they didn't give a shit about me either, and I learned not to give a shit about any of them. I walked right past his open hands and into Angie's. Her church music was blasting, as it usually is when she's cleaning.

"Nigga I blew your phone up! Fuck you been at!" yelled Nick, his big jaws dribbled straight at me.

"Almost getting killed! Calm the fuck down! Angie! Go get some alcohol for me!" She couldn't hear over the music.

"Angie! Get me some alcohol!"

"Boy, get you some alcohol what!" Angie yelled, cutting the music off.

"Please! Get me some alcohol please!"

"Okay, baby!" she answered from upstairs.

"My bad, Dee," said Nick, "and bring a cold rag too, Angie! Please! This nigga all bloody! Anyway, Ike got us for like thirty-five hundred dollars, fifteen hundred pills, Yo. I'm sorry."

"What the fuck? Fifteen hundred? Why you running around with that? You out your fucking mind! Nigga, you paying that shit back!"

Nick said he had a date and couldn't make the re-up. I was ready to tell him how stupid he was but Angie walked down stairs with a beige hand towel and some peroxide.

"Ohhh, are you okay, baby? You get Li'l Bo and Tay get a bail yet?"

"What?"

"Yeah, Dee. Fat Tay and Li'l Bo got bagged. We gotta bail them out. We need help on this corner, you don't be up here enough. And I don't really know what's up with Block. He ain't even show up today."

I wasn't trying to hear any of that bullshit Nick was saying. Long Tooth was down and someone really shot me, well, slightly grazed me, but that shit still hurt. I looked down at my phone. Soni and Troy had both called me a bunch of times.

"Yo, we gotta get ready for war, man. You ready for this, right!" Nick declared, slamming his revolver on the table. "People talkin' about you and that car, people talkin' about our block, niggas is comin' at us. So we gotta do something. I don't mind paying the money I owe, but we gotta do something."

"You right," I said, giving Nick a pound and heading back to my crib. I ignored my phone for the rest of night, swallowed three Perks, drowned a pint of Grey Goose, and fell out.

BYE, DEE

A few days later, I dialed Soni. Her voice was a song—bright enough to light up pitch-dark nights while soothing enough to ease any pain, especially mine. She was as soft and gentle as her voice but still—her words could move worlds.

"Hey, stranger! Where have you been?" she said. "I missed you."

"Hey, Soni. I wasn't being a stranger, I was almost shot the other day. Had nothing to do with me, though, well, not really, so don't worry."

"Not really? That sounds stupid! I can't tell you that you don't belong out there if you can't see it yourself, Dee. Get off of my phone, and finish throwing your life away!"

Click!

I dialed her back like eight times. I was sent straight to her voice mail eight times.

Soni was an important part of my life. She's the one. I had to figure out a way to fix it. I didn't know who I could talk to for advice, so I called my mom.

"Long time, son, how are you? Back in school yet?"

"Naw, mom, I need to ask you a question."

She said she had to click over and cancel her other call because she knew it was serious. I never really call or visit. I think about her, but I know that no mom wants a drug-dealing son so I try to keep my distance.

"Okay, son, what's wrong?"

"I like a girl and I think I broke her heart."

"Well, Dee, you need to just pray on it. Ask God to lead you in the right direction. I'ma come see you on Sunday, it's been too long!"

"Come through the park on Sunday morning, I'll be out!"

We said I love you and hung up. Always pray and always ask God. I don't really know how to talk to my mom. She used to be a seven-day-a-week partying club queen but now she's a religious zealot and answers every question with a praise or a Bible quote. I understand church guides her, but I wished we could just rap without her busting into a mini-sermon.

MY RELIGION

I do believe in God," I said.

Fixing my two platinum chains—one slightly longer than the other with two-toned Jesus heads attached to each. I hated when they tangled.

"Don't you ever question my religion; Jesus hangs on my neck twice!" I said laughingly to my mom, who stood over me with loud eyes and a twisted lip—her neck was cocked east with the rest of her body leaning west.

I was sitting on the park bench over Ellwood where I asked her to meet me. Sometimes I wasted Sundays feeding pigeons, blowing weed circles, and trading war stories with some dope fiends from my neighborhood.

My mom was church ready. She looked royal—fuchsia form-fitting dress offset by a huge purse. Her shoes and Sunday crown matched.

"I know you believe in God, Dee, so come to church!" she pleaded.

I'd rather eat used tampons, is what I thought; "I'll pass" is what I said. I never spent too much time in churches, but I know "Church Folk"—I can't really comprehend them.

Church Folk are thirty- to fifty-something, slightly over-weight, and programmed to be judgmental. Most are broke but a few are paid, with some middle-class people sprinkled in—the seating chart is donation-based, meaning that the elite sit in the front and the bottom-feeders are lucky if they can peek in through the back window. They all gather for approximately twelve hours every Sunday to praise God.

God is neither the Kenny Rogers–looking guy that Michelangelo conceptualized, or the Isaac Hayes rendition that emerged from the black community.

God to "Church Folk" is the Kool-Aid-red robe-wearing, $100,000 car driving, Jheri Curl glistening, central incisor gold tooth having, gator-skin boot sporting with two fists full of gleaming fourteen-karat rings dude—slanging globs of praise and spit from the throne in the pulpit every Sunday, always playing the saint when he's really more crooked than a meth fiend's smile.

Fuck listening to that guy. Most of the fake prophets only focus on profits. Congregation members who struggle to pay their light bills wouldn't dare ask the church for a loan, and if they did, the only answer they would probably receive is "I can't give you money but we can pray on it!"

Multiple hardship stories like this in combination with what I heard about the infinite number of boy-lusting Catholic priests who hang around Boy Scout conventions and in the back of Toys R Us made me question organized religion.

"Church ain't really for me, Mom."

"All churches aren't the same, Dee. You need to give mine a chance. I'll save you a seat!" she said as she hopped in her car and peeled off.

I didn't answer. She knew I wasn't coming just like I knew she wasn't saving me a seat. Just like me, my mother is a serial escapist, and she just used the church scene to replace the nightclubs—same thing, if you think about it. Flashy cars, money flowing, addictive music, excessive fucking, and respect based on financial status.

Soni always rapped about how the religions we celebrate were used as tools for implementing genocide, colonization, and the enslavement of people across the globe, but I don't blame God. The fundamentals of these religious practices are great but the people—the people fuck them up, leaving me to separate myself from them and develop my own understanding of what God is.

Orgasms, an exotic marijuana buzz, the smirk on my homie's face when his ten-pound son popped out of his lady's vagina, the feeling you get when you are starving and the waiter arrives with your appetizer, or the warmth that shoots through you after a good-bye kiss from your love at the airport make the existence of a higher power undeniable.

We have the power to create our own realities. People who chase and catch their dreams are in heaven while the others who travail daily in a hate-packed existence reside in hell.

My mom had her heaven and I had mine.

And in the midst of her trying to bring me to her heaven, I got zero advice on reconnecting with Soni.

SOME NEW SHIT WILL FIX IT

I couldn't stop thinking about Soni, her eyes and her spirit. We could run away and be like the Cosbys or that family from the *Fresh Prince*, with beautiful kids, good credit, clear healthy skin, and a nice home. I could live off of my street money and re-enroll in college while she finished up and found a grad school. We could be those elite blacks who never forgot where we came from. The ones who come back to the hood to give out books and throw block parties.

My daydream was interrupted by a call from Tone. He said that Fat Tay had a bail on the drug charge he had got booked for, but I said fuck him. Let him sit forever, it's time for me to tighten up. I was knee-deep in this shit and I had money, enough money for me to pick and choose who I wanted around me.

Li'l Bo was still sitting. Tone told me that his girlfriend said they are violating his probation so he might not get bail. I told him she could come by later and get three thousand for the lawyer. Li'l Bo probably had that in his stash, but fuck it—I take care of the people I love.

Ring ring ring . . .

"Block, what's up? Where you at, dummy?"

"Down the projects, come get me."

"Ten minutes."

Block was down at Somerset Homes; a lot of my family and friends were from down there. Driving through those courts brought me back to some of my best moments—Miss Rita's frozen cups, playing catch one, catch all with my friends, my first kiss with Jasmine, cutting school and smoking jays with Damon and Smoke, dance contests, funky underwear smelling house parties, walking over to Toi's for a slice of pizza, laughing at how hard we laughed, being a kid. I'll always love that place. Block was already on the corner waiting for me.

"Yo, you ready to kill something for real?" asked Block, getting in, slamming my door way too hard. He pulled a .45 off of his waist and flashed it. "Man, they fucked with the wrong niggas!"

"Yo, watch the door, clown! And naw. We gotta get with Dog Boy later. Relax on that beef shit, man. I'll figure it out. It has to be done right. LT's alive, meaning that making money is still the number one thing we need to concern ourselves with."

"Won't be no money if we all dead, but Yooooo! Gee super mad! He heard about that shit, boy, he ready! I promised he had the big sawed-off shotgun on him down here late night!"

I knew I could always count on Gee for gunplay, but I wasn't thinking about war, or why Block wasn't coming to work, or anything but LT's health, Soni's smile, and fucking some money up. I needed to show the hood how much I appreciated them. Greedy dudes who flash money and Benzs without giving back get big gaping bulletholes in their heads.

I pulled a well-twisted rello from behind my ear.

"Spark this, we goin' shoppin." Block's eyes lit like the Bic lighter he used to spark the rello. I wasn't sure if he was more excited over the weed or the new shit I was about to buy.

* * *

Spending money's great for depression. As street dudes, it's all we really have. America's racist as fuck and businesses do everything in their power to keep black people out of the workforce. My cousin Jaquan said he couldn't get a callback for a job until he started putting Jay as his first name on applications. To make matters worse, our country has laws that force companies to interview blacks, furthering the point that they don't want to see us make it anyway. We felt like we'd never have great careers or huge homes—the only happiness we find lies in these luxury items we keep buying.

Soni says chanting will remove my negative energy. I tried to do it with her, it didn't work—but spending, spending works. Spending's a way for me to channel that negative energy into some positive thoughts. I had a nice Benz, about fifteen thousand dollars on me in tens and twenties, plus a big-ass empty trunk that needed to be filled up. Life was good. USA Boutique—the hood version of Macy's at Mondawmin Mall—was the first stop. We call it the hood Macy's because they carry designer brands like Polo in the big sizes we liked to rock.

Stores like the Boutique, RudoSports from back in the day, and DTLR made Mondawmin one of the top cash malls in the country. They carried the clothes that clothed the dope dealers. Nikes, Rocawear, Polo, Sergio, Maurice Malone, Sean Jean, Mecca, ENYCE, Guess, Evisu, Hilfiger, Adidas, Boss, Lacoste, Puma, Nautica, New Balance, Prada, Air Jordans, True Religion, Timberland, and a bunch of other shit—I bought it all.

Sammy, one of the owners, greeted us at the door with a pound. "How you been, man?"

I dapped him back and said, "Living." From there, two girls

followed us around the store as we pulled everything Polo and Lacoste off of the racks—hoodies, shirts, sweaters, buckets, t-shirts, everything. I needed to make sure I had a huge care package for LT because he took that bullet, and some designer shit for Angie because she works for me and can't be going to church looking all raggedy, and a leather coat for Dog Boy just because, plus some ill shit for Lil Bo to wear to court, and some husky clothes for Nick because he's getting fatter by the second, and probably some pink or purple shit for Tone—he never leaves his crib, but I know he likes to walk around the house with new clothes on. We piled so much stuff on the girls that you could no longer see their faces; their arms were tired, and they had to make trips back and forth to the countertop.

I gave Block some stacks. "Cash them out, Yo, I'm gonna get us some tennis!"

I wasn't sure what sizes everybody wore but it was fall and my people needed boots, even Kruger Man. He washed my car with holey shoes that are funky like PCP smoke, and it was about to be too cold for that, plus I didn't want the smell to get on me or in my car. I bought a bunch of Timberlands—different shades, different colors, and different sizes. Didn't really matter who could fit them or not, I'd just park on Madeira, pop my trunk and give them all away.

"My man, the Jordan 3 Retros drop on Saturday. Slip me a extra hundred, you can get them now," said a salesman.

"Yo, I need like fifteen pair, I'll give you an extra thousand over the price."

"I could lose my job, man! How about three pair?" he bargained.

I should live. My family should live. "Yo, fifteen hundred plus the price, man, load me up, G. Plus I wanna buy everybody in the store a pair of shoes!"

"Damn, man, you need some shoe cleaner for all of those kicks? I'll throw some free ones in!"

"Thanks, man, but you can give them to the people who want them. I don't really clean my shoes, I just get new ones."

There were about fifteen people in the store walking away with something free because of me. I cashed the kid out. He helped carry the boxes to my car and we stuffed them in the back. Block was still in the mall buying more stuff. I went back to get him and passed a jewelry store. There was a platinum and diamond bracelet in the window. Soni probably wouldn't wear it but fuck it, if she didn't I'd give it to my mom or just have crazy store credit—I dropped another $3K on the bracelet, met Block and our ten thousand bags, then shot back down Madeira Street.

I gave away more than I kept. Everybody in my crew had Jordan 3's before they came out, even Miss Angie. She rocked hers with a flower-printed muumuu while running around in the kitchen making us lunch. Her fat ankles bulged out of the sides—the front of them creased the first half hour she owned them. I never saw Jordans fuck up so quickly.

That night, Angie made a big-ass dinner and we all ate. Everybody was fresh. Kruger looked really funny with a new jacket, new boots, and old-ass clothes from the late eighties underneath. Nick and Dog Boy pulled up in a new green Range Rover with stickers tattooed to every window.

"Oh shit!" we said. "Look at these niggas!" was yelled in different tones while everybody ambushed the truck like steak in a piranha tank.

4.0?

Nick's new truck had paper tags and new rims. It was a used Range Rover to somebody, but new to us. Whirlwinds of weed smoke exited the car before Dog Boy and Nick jumped out. "You keep the Lexus? You keep the Lexus?" was the number one question for two reasons. One: everybody was nosy and wanted to see how much money we really had. Two: dudes thought they could borrow the Lex while he drove the Range or borrow the Range while he drove the Lex.

"Naw, dug, I keep all my whips! And y'all ugly asses ain't driving them!" yelled Nick, beating on his chest like a gorilla. Nick liked to beat on his chest when he accomplished a goal, or when he was trying to make a point about something—basically whenever he was in his feelings.

"You really need two luxury cars?" I asked as I surveyed the vehicle, checking out the rims, thinking about how crazy it was that we had a Lex, a Benz, and a Range in the crew—we were really moving work.

"Is you really hatin'?" he replied in a gulp of a chuckle. I laughed; we all did until I stopped. I had to.

The rear of the truck fucked up my day. It read "4.0."

"Really, Nick? A 4.0? What the fuck is wrong with you!" Everybody on the block jumped in like "Hell no! Take that shit back, boy! That cheap-ass truck!"

"What? I saved ten racks! What the fuck!" Nick argued.

I ain't give a shit. The hood ain't give a shit. We wasn't having that. We are students of Jay culture, direct products of Jay-Zism—meaning that anything under a 4.6 is unacceptable. Jay Z even had a whole song called "Imaginary Player" where he clowns a dude for driving a 4.0, telling him to spend that thirty G's, so fuck that. I wasn't going to let Nick go out like that.

"Nick! Building up these haters was hard work! You can't let them off the hook with a 4.0!" I yelled. Some guys laughed, but I was serious as cancer in its final stage. We took our Jay Z shit seriously, meaning that we didn't even wear fake stuff. We couldn't drive small economy luxury vehicles like 3 series Beamers, we didn't drink rail vodka, our jewelry was platinum, Cristal was the only champagne for us, we carried packs of Franklins because Washingtons were a no-no, and we didn't put aftermarket diamonds in our Rolex watches because that's uncivilized, plus it cheapened the value.

No one from our hood really knew the difference between a 4.0 and 4.6. Some of the dudes who joined me in clowning Nick's truck didn't even have cars. Some of them couldn't even get their hands on a hundred dollars and others were junkies who lived in places without running water. Some were kids and most of us were from public housing but Jay Z set the standard and we rolled with it.

Nick took the truck back the next morning and came around with a shiny black 4.6 with twenty-inch black rims to match. The streets went crazy. I started hearing wild rumors like our cars were rented and our money came from us receiving settlements due to lead paint poisoning. Some of us had lead but our new money didn't come from checks.

I laughed at it all and spent more.

SHOULD'VE

We were beyond stupid. We should've laid back. We were facing a war and just kept buying shit. Shit and more shit. My whole hood was fresh from head to toe—it looked like a Macy's and a Foot Locker warehouse had exploded.

I shouldn't say *we*. I was the boss, so I should take personal responsibility.

I should've been protecting my crew, loading up on weapons, recruiting soldiers, doing pull-ups, applying war paint under my eyes, and mapping out strategic attack plans on a dry-erase board in a room full of killers. I should've been kneeling over the edge of my bed every night, cleaning off my nickel-plated .45—checking my reflection, and anticipating the kill. I should've been doing research on those kids in the Taurus and making sure my strips pumped cash because you can't have a war without money.

Soni should've not known a thing about the shooting or LT's wound, but that's impossible because pain goes straight to my face, so she would've found out eventually. I should've known that she'd hear my story, call me crazy, and leave. I should've mastered a poker face by now. Shutting the fuck up when talking to women about street shit is an OG rule. I should've known not to break it.

I should've been excited about avenging LT, Dog Boy, and myself. I should've called Hurk up and invited him to a meeting with Uncle Gee because they are the most bloodthirsty people I know. But I didn't even tell them. I should've been visualizing bullets ripping through the flesh of the kids that shot at us, watching their blood spill and laughing all the while.

I should've been able to trash the smoking pistol, bop into LT's hospital room and say, "You should've seen their faces when I caught them! I laid them out and gave them all headshots, just for li'l bro! You ain't gotta hurt no more!"

He should've been able to take a deep pull of the oxygen, smile and say, "You should've waited for me. I like to get my hands dirty, big bro."

We should've both known that trying to hurt the people who hurt us wouldn't heal that hole in this chest.

We should've known, but we were beyond stupid.

OLD HEAD SAID

Troy hit my phone like two millions times in one day, saying, "Mr. Pete needs to see you! Go talk to him now! Please!"

I silenced Troy and headed Mr. Pete's way ASAP. I didn't go just because he was our connect. He also gave me crazy game and countless lessons—lessons that got deeper with every trip, shit every young person needs to know. Gems to live by were buried in all of his rants. After my two months' worth of trips to the dialysis unit, I was finally used to the funky formaldehyde smell that stuck to my clothes like chewed gum. The cute secretary, Robin, knew me now; she even buzzed me into the clinic without Troy. I knew my way around the unit—enough to reach Mr. Pete.

He was propped back as usual, watching *The Price Is Right* and winning. Pete was way better at estimating the price of the trips and cars offered than the screaming housewives that ran up and down the aisle on the show each day.

"OG, wassup?" I said, propping myself on a beige leather stool and rolling in his direction. He took his earphones off and waved me closer. I inched forward. He waved again, this time positioning himself close enough to whisper in my ear. "Dee," he said, "you are going to die if you don't get off those streets. The next bullet will hit your head, boy. I promise. I dun seen plenty of li'l dudes like you get flipped, easy."

161

I sat still, looking down at my feet for a minute, and then tried to pick up my head enough to look Pete in the eye. It felt like a ten-thousand-pound weight was on the back of my neck. Pete rolled his eyes and leaned back in his chair, looking at me in despair. He shook his head in shame and turned his nose up as if I wasn't worth spitting on.

"I hate your generation," he mumbled. "Fuckin' crack babies."

"I'm confused," I said.

He didn't reply; some doctors had walked behind me and were checking his machine. The unit's charge nurse pushed some buttons and flicked some switches.

"Howdy, Mr. Pete! Have you been taking all of your medicine and watching your fluids?" a block-headed young doctor asked; he looked fresh out of med school.

Pete shrugged and said, "I'm here and alive right?"

The nurse called Pete cranky and laughed it off. They caved to doctors and cringe when patients didn't do the same. The duo continued to make their rounds throughout the clinic.

"So Troy told you about the shooting, huh?"

Pete said it wasn't just the shooting. He wanted to know why was I living in the city because he was from an era where black dope dealers got rich and moved to Randallstown. "You aren't supposed to eat where you shit, boy," he said. That meant I should slang in east Baltimore and live way out in the county—I knew that but I couldn't. I love east Baltimore and I ain't never leaving; plus, I have a apartment downtown, I just like to hang on my block—but that wasn't good enough for him. I laughed and said, "Hell no! Maybe in the nineties! Rich niggas move to Atlanta now!" Pete didn't find it funny.

"Why y'all on blocks anyway?" he whispered. His lips were

really chapped, and cotton grew at the seams, enough to stuff a case of aspirin bottles. I felt his pressure rise.

"I know you have lead, but I think you are smart enough to know that wholesaling is the only way. That block shit is over, boy. You should be shot dead by now. You and Troy are in a good position to make some money and start a business. Drugs ain't forever. Ain't no 401K for smack dealers, boy. You lucky you not dead!"

I thought about the shootouts, Ike Guy and the rest of the racist cops that beat on us. I thought about Long Tooth, when he was coming out of the hospital and would he ever be the same. Bip. I thought of Bip. I thought about Li'l Bo and Fat Tay in jail—what if I was next? Could I even deal with that shit? I thought about how I hated working on the block. I didn't mind sitting out and joking with my friends and the junkies, but working was a hassle. I've spent eighteen hours plus in the same spot on multiple days. How long could I sit there and collect money with no war? War was guaranteed like death and taxes. How long would the cops allow guns to be our get out of jail free cards? Madeira Street would end soon, just like it ended before. Everybody knew us; even the cops. We all looked liked a bunch of targets out there anyway, waiting to get plucked off. It could happen any day.

"Mr. Pete, look, man..."

"Shut up—when your mouth is open, your ears are closed!"

I paused. The streets forced me to not respect many, but Pete was genuine.

"I used to run Pennsylvania Avenue back in the day, boy. I told you that, no, listen. Me and some real gangstas had some night spots. We ran a big dawg card game upstairs and performances in the lounges downstairs. We booked everybody and when I say everybody, I mean everybody from Billie Holiday to Nat King

Cole. When the biggest stars weren't performing, they were in my clubs, having a drink and living that life. Redd Foxx came through, Satchmo came through, Duke came through, everybody, man, we ran the most classy joints on this side of the Mason-Dixon. The gangsters mixed and mingled with the artists. The most beautiful women in the whole city would come out every night! Boy, I tell you we had something beautiful. Something real!" He gazed as he reminisced. His eyes glossed; he rubbed his belly as if it was full and laid his head back in the chair. His machine went off. One of the nurse techs came by to adjust it.

"Really? It looks like *Night of the Living Dead* out there now, I even be hittin' workers over there with bundles and weight. What happened, Mr. Pete?"

"We happened. We let it go, boy. We let it go without a care. I was young and dumb like you. I let greed fuel me. I could move that dope. That dope money looked way better than that club money and we led a lot of our clientele straight to it." Pete sat up and looked me in the eyes. "That was the worst shit I ever done. Look at me, boy. Smart people learn from they own mistakes. Genius niggas learn from other people's mistakes. Make your wholesale money while I can get what I can get you. Get off the block and start a legit business. Go to a college like Troy. I wanna see you boys do good, better than us. Don't try to do this shit forever, you aint me and things aint the same." Pete leaned back in his chair. I sat there in military silence and thought about what he said. I knew Soni would agree. Pete was right, that block shit was stupid, but what about my crew? Who's going take care of Tone? What about Angie and everything I worked to build?

I thought all about the people I fed in that neighborhood. The kids who needed a little extra money for school, the junkies who needed a little help getting high, the junkies who needed a little help getting clean, the coaches, the church niggas, the pretty girls, the up and coming athletes, the single moms—I fed them all, at some point.

Mr. Pete's three-hour session had ended and I left the unit. Madeira Street was still wrapped all around my mind. The lives of the block residents like Mr. Sam played in my head like movies. Mr. Sam had a wife and some kids who all looked liked him. He knew me from the days he sold coke with my uncle Gee. Sam caught a small bit and vowed to never hustle again after his release. Even though he wore soiled work clothes everyday, he was always in between jobs, and I used to give him a couple of dollars here and there. I never did it in front of anyone. It had to be in private because he was the man of his house and no one needed to see him relying on me. Being a provider was important to him and he didn't want his kids to see him taking or borrowing money from a dealer. I respected him for trying to break that cycle, and he always paid me back, even when I tried not to take it. As I laid out my next move, I realized that the people meant more to me than the money. I was an important part of a community and it would cause a major impact if I just removed myself from the equation.

But I wouldn't really be able to do anything for anybody if I was dead or in jail. Mr. Pete was right; I was falling victim to the same greed that got him. That's the reason he has all of that money and is still unhappy about a lot of things. He wears a Rolex made of diamonds, everyone at the unit kisses his ass, and I heard his house had eight bedrooms with a sick pool—but still, his happiest days came from running a legit club with good music. His happiness came from happy people.

I knew then, I was done with Madeira Street.

STRAIGHT TO VOICE MAIL

I dialed Soni, and it went straight to voice mail, again. But she had to be the first to know that my days on Madeira Street were over. I was going to get off the block, get my health in order, and start a business—just like Mr. Pete had. I had zero credit but my car was paid for, I had a half a brick of dope to split with Troy with more to come from Pete, and about $200K saved up.

Call from Hurk: sent to voice mail.

Running a convenience store couldn't be that hard. I bought and sold dope all of the time. I got fronted and paid back. I paid my crew, I paid my debts, stacked buy money, shopped weekly and still had dough left over to save. People don't shoot at storeowners, well, not normally. And if it all fails, I'd still have dope to sell as a wholesaler until Pete stopped.

Call from Hurk: sent to voice mail.

Nick would be able to hold Madeira Street down. He'd been doing that anyway but now all the extra money could go to him and whatever worker he decided to pick up. Even calling myself a wholesaler felt better than being married to a block. I couldn't even believe I did that shit for so long. I had to tell Soni, but she was avoiding me like I was avoiding Hurk.

After three days of missed calls, I decided to drive to her mom's house. I had just picked Long Tooth up from Johns Hopkins, which was a few blocks away. Long Tooth had Perks and vodka. He leaned sideways in the passenger seat and dozed off, only waking when I cut Lil Boosie off. He'd pop up and say, "Pump the Boosie, man! We need dat! Going through some thangs! I swear for God, Boosie the one!"

I pulled onto the corner adjacent to Soni's mom's house. "Glad you back, LT, I love you, li'l bro. Tell me what you want, I'll get you whatever you want, I mean that!" Long Tooth sat up straight and turned the beat down, and our eyes met: "I want some more pills, I want my dick sucked by a Destiny's Child girl—any one of dem—and I want us to kill dem niggas dat shot me, all of dem." He leaned back in the chair, took a swig of Goose, and closed his eyes.

"Really, Dee, I just want them niggas got."

I took a roll of cash out of my pocket and sat it in the cup holder. "Well, this ain't enough money to get head from a Destiny's Child girl but I bet you could fuck they friends." He cracked a smile. Soni's car was parked out front so I exited with the bracelet I bought her and knocked on her door. She poked her head out of the window.

"Stalker! What do you want!" She laughed. "Do you understand English?"

"I'm not on the street anymore, can we rap about it later?" I yelled. Long Tooth watched from the car shaking his head, looking at me like I was crazy. Soni came downstairs and opened the door. I waved that one *I'll be right back* finger at Long Tooth before walking in. Her mom's house smelled like perfume and turkey wings.

"Are you lying to me?" she asked.

I wrapped my arms around her. "I've been thinking, I'm tired of this shit. I bought you a gift." I kept my left arm around her waist and pulled the bracelet out of my pocket with the right.

"It's platinum and diamond, I hope you like it."

"Oh, my God, it's so pretty! Are these conflict-free diamonds?"

"Absolutely!"

"No, they aren't!" she said, pushing the bracelet back at me. "I should cash that thing in and pay my student loans off! No, but really, it's really nice. I can't take it. I really like you. I don't want gifts; I only want you as a safe, like a square that doesn't run the streets. Can that be my gift?"

I put the box back in my pocket. "You mean like a dashiki-wearing nigga with dreads and open-toe sandals?"

She laughed. "No, silly, just you without the crime. I love you." She stood on her tippy-toes and kissed my lips. I dipped down and stole another kiss when she pulled away.

"I love you too, Soni."

MURDER TEAM

Madeira Street was a ghost town. My shop was closed; Nick sat on Angie's steps in all black. His hood eclipsed his eyes, his back lined up with the wall; his head was like a swivel rotating in every direction—he was on point. I parked and joined him.

"Yo, wassup?" I asked.

"You gotta gun on you?" said Nick, still looking over my shoulder and surveying the block.

"Naw," I replied, trying to follow his eyes and see what he was looking for.

"Yo, you talk to Hurk? Sit by me and hold this," he said, passing me a Glock.

"Naw, I ain't rap to Hurk," I replied. Nick told me that someone shot Rex up and Hurk has been coming through every hour on the hour looking for me.

"Damn, is he dead?"

"I don't even know, man, but he buggin' out and that's not even the worse part. Dis day fucked!" he said.

"It gets worse?" I asked.

Nick nodded and said that Gee hooked up with Long Tooth and picked up Dog Boy. The trio popped handfuls of ecstasy and had been riding around the city all day shooting at any and everyone they thought had something to do with our incident. No one had asked me or gave a fuck what I thought. They waged a war off of blindness—with Gee, who has never made a rational decision in his life. I'm not even sure who told him about the shooting, but the idea of me being attacked probably sent him crazy. Especially since I put him back on his feet. I love him but he is the definition of what no one should ever aim to be like. Gee also had a million petty charges, ranging from domestics to assault.

Gee once climbed into the booth and knocked out the DJ at Strawberries for not playing DMX. Afterward he threw the guy into the crowd and took over the show. When I was a kid he rode a dirt bike wearing nothing but a blue mink and some blue gators all through his project lobby—old women turned away and covered their kids' eyes. The housing cops managed to tackle him off of the bike but he knocked out a few before they subdued him, and he did the shit again as soon as he got a bail. Gee's never been sober, and his gun stays warm; he doesn't fuck with vegetables—he doesn't really fuck with anything. Forever he'll be a wildcard with no filter; he'll always drink life and smoke whatever you pass to him. He always made every situation worse.

"Yo, you got extra bullets?" I asked. Nick was right, I needed a gun; I'm not getting killed because of their bullshit. Nick said he had a case at the crib. I texted Soni, *I love you* just because. Hurk had pulled up in a new CL500 with his passenger window down.

"Dee, ya phone broke, nigga? Get in the car, man."

Soni texted *I love you* back. I dapped Nick and hopped in Hurk's ride. The interior was a rich peanut butter color and smelled like new leather dipped in weed smoke and a vanilla tree. Hennessy leaped out of his pores. We cut through Bradford and rode up Monument Street. Nick wasn't lying, nobody was out. This Gee shit was all my fault. I should've handled this situation before LT came out. We could've spent a month in the islands. By the time we would've returned, they wouldn't care about this petty beef shit. Hurk had a Mac 11 in his lap with an extended clip poking out. There was a sawed-off shotgun with peeling grip tape on the handle resting in the backseat. I saw the bulletproof vest print all in his t-shirt.

"Where we going at?" I asked.

"Nowhere for real, just wanna put you down with Rex. Niggas tryin' to say we killed him, that's crazy shit, right?"

"We! Fuck you mean 'we'?"

He said he was as surprised as me and that I needed to lay low for a while. He needed some time to figure everything out because it was a strong possibility that some people would be coming for us. This is the ugly part of the game that recruiters forget to mention—home invasions, sleepless nights, gun battles, and wondering if you'll be the next person with a hole in your head or in a wheelchair or dead. We pulled up at a 7-Eleven. Some people admired the car.

"What you want, Yo?" asked Hurk.

"Grab me an extra large red Slurpee and some seeds!" I yelled out the window. A frail shell of a woman approached the car.

"Can I have some change please?"

I glanced at her round face and patted my pockets. The only thing worse than her skin and breath were her teeth—they were jagged and spotted like dice. A cloud of crack funk followed her. I glanced again. It was Hope. Hope was a junkie now. I pulled some crumbled ones from a roll of money I had tucked in my sock. She didn't acknowledge me and I didn't acknowledge her.

"Aye, get the fuck away from my car, you stinky bitch!" yelled Hurk, coming out of the store.

"It's cool!" I said. "It's cool"

She tucked her head down and walked away. Hurk threw his fountain soda in her direction, cranked his Project Pat album, and skidded off.

I looked at myself in the side-view mirror. The reflection had red eyes like hers, rough skin like hers—my tone was off, I looked numb. I didn't look as good as I thought I did. I could be Hope sometime soon.

Fuck that!

Dear Percocets,

I can't even front, we had some amazing times together. Met you at eighteen and now I'm twenty! Who thought I'd see twenty! You've been there when I couldn't even buy a friend, helping me get over death after death after death, and letdown after letdown after letdown—numbing me to the pain of life. You made everything better, which makes this painful, but I gotta let you go. I'll always love you, but you gotta go.

You fucking my hood up, my friends up, and fucking me up too. We all look ugly and ten years older because of you. I keep shitting blood and I know it's because of you; I act like it's not but I know it's you. You are on my mind all the time and it's messed up how all of the bad things always have to be so damn good. You, raw pussy, and chocolate chip cookies are all bad but you all feel so good.

I was riding through my block the other day and you were out. I knew you were out because you all over east Baltimore now, on every stoop, project lobby, and corner. Dudes who used to be the cleanest are walking around with holey Nikes, mini linty 'fros, and

173

shredded-worn Seven jeans. They keep scratching like they are covered in ants and so do I. They are the new junkies and I'm one of them.

I saw a respected hustler get bitched by a heroin addict over you the other day. It felt like I was in the *Twilight Zone.* I couldn't tell who the junkie was because the hustler needed you as much as the heroin addict needed his heroin. They were both sick. I'm sick and I don't want to be anymore, so you gotta go.

I don't want to sell drugs forever so it's definitely time to stop using them. Thank you for everything. I'll always remember you. Bulletproof love.

Your homie,

Dee

HOT BOY TROY

I wanted to rap to Troy about my issues with Hurk so I headed to his place.

Troy's family moved to Decker Street, about a block away from the top of Ellwood Park. His room was in the basement. Their walls were cluttered with family pictures from back in the day. Big afros in front of Cadillacs, party shots, his parents inside of champagne glasses and heart-shaped frames, Troy's Little League baseball cards and a bunch of prom portraits—Jheri Curls and gold teeth were on every image. His mom greeted me like, "Heyyyyyy baby," as always before saying, "He down that basement. You hungry? Lemme know, baby, cuz you thin! I'll fry you sumthin'!"

I thanked her, declined the food, and dipped my head so that I wouldn't hit it while walking down the basement stairs. I almost tripped over the collage of sneaker boxes that blanketed the floor. Troy wasn't a sneaker guy but I guessed hustling was changing him too—he had everything, everywhere from Gucci to Reebok to brands I never even heard of.

"Troy, what's up, man?"

"I'm great, bro, I just scrambled and put together a hundred fifty grams for us, time to knock these off!" he said, tossing the work on his bed next to a bunch of new shirts and hats. "I got some plays for us out of town too, Dee, as soon as Mr. Pete get us that new shit!"

"Damn, man, you trying to open a clothing store? I thought I had too much shit!" I said, moving some shirts and sitting down. "Yo, I feel kind of bad, man, I gotta rap to you about something serious."

Troy opened the storm window and sparked a blunt.

"Yo, you a rich nigga, you ain't got no problems; shit, I'm trying get like you so I can have your problems!" he said, passing me the blunt. "But yoooooo, I don't fuck with Kim no more! Why this bitch say she wanted to do a threesome and I was like hell-to-the- yeah! So I booked the nice hotel and she showed up looking good as shit! I was like it's on nigga and then asked where her friend at. She said he on his way and I said what! Sure enough, dude knocked on the door, and I put both of they dumbasses out!"

I choked on the weed and then choked even harder on Troy's story. He gave me a break from the bullshit that Hurk hit me with. In that moment I didn't feel scared. Troy went on for another hour about women and money and then women and more money. He never doubled back around to ask if I was cool or not. Troy didn't even sound like Troy. The game has a way of doing this. The game takes innocent kids like us and transforms us. Two loving guys with big hearts who were supposed to never hustle, sitting here talking about nothing but hustling and girls and hustling again.

I couldn't even tell him what I was going through. He just assumed that I had no issues—that we had no issues because we were making a couple of dollars. Troy said nothing about college or starting a business. His only concerns were who he was fucking next and how much heroin we had to sell.

"Dee, I'm buying a Beamer too! A 745—please be aware that every girl in the state of Maryland will want to suck my dick!"

"I hope it makes you happy," I replied. Leaning back on the bed looking at the full zip of heroin: "I hope it makes you happy."

NICK GOT THE BLOCK

The fifteen-minute ride from my condo at the Green House down to Nick's spot felt like a ten-hour road trip. Probably because I couldn't imagine not being connected to Madeira Street, and I was worried about what Nick would say. We came into this together and I didn't want to abandon him, but it had to be done. Selling drugs outside is like being a fish in a bowl—everybody can watch your every move and you can't do anything about it. I wasn't going to die on that block and I figured I'd let him make his own decision.

Some dope fiends were cleaning his truck with suds and ripped-up t-shirts when I pulled up. He added big gaudy wheels to his Range, they had to be twenty-two inches or more. Small diamond-like crystals circled the base; I guess they made for a better shine. I walked up to them and touched the tip—it spun around slow like a ceiling fan.

"What in the fuck?" I said, spinning them hard, like a game show contestant.

"Yeah, buddy, he ridin' spinners! When you stop, dey keep goin'! Twenty-five thousand dollar wheels, Nick say dey cost, you gotta get some, Dee!" said the guy cleaning them. He was a new fiend; I didn't know him. He knew my name and my job and I couldn't pick him out of a lineup. All of these dudes suffer from what I call "The Fifth Nigga Syndrome," meaning that the story always gets stretched all the way out of shape by the time it reaches the fifth nigga. Twenty-five thousand dollars in the hood means about six thousand in real life. I never subscribe to Fifth Nigga Syndrome, but either way, the resale value was probably two pennies and those wheels looked stupid to me, like rolling indictments. Seeing those pointless attention suckers made me feel a little better about my decision, and then breaking away from these strangers further validated what I was already thinking. I told the fiend to get my car next and walked into the house. Li'l Bo sent us mail and a picture of him kneeling in standard gray DOC sweats that read, "Stay up, my niggas! Death B4 Dishonor" on the back.

The house smelled like a crack rock outlet. I told Nick to stop frying in the crib at least two million times but he was too fat and lazy to pack the work at our stash house. His clothes were all over the place. It's like he stripped, changed, and just left the shit on the couch, floor, and everywhere else.

"You sloppy as shit!" I yelled.

Every day he wrapped himself in State Property gear and cranked the *State Property* CD on the highest level. I loved that album but never really understood that clothing line. It was created by the rapper Beanie Sigel from Philly. Every shirt, jacket, and jumpsuit was designed to make you look like an inmate. Like going to jail was cool. Li'l Bo had to wear that shit and I'm sure he wouldn't rock those clothes if he were free. Some of the shirts even had fake prison ID numbers printed on front—I'm surprised those clown suits didn't come with fake cuffs. I loved that all those rap dudes were busting out with clothing lines but fuck, a jail look— plus my days of urban apparel were fading. I was switching to wholesaling, which meant I needed to look the part. Wholesalers should live in designers like Gucci and Loui, or at least that's what I thought.

Every fly in east Baltimore lived in Nick's kitchen. I had fiends cleaning the place twice a week when I stayed there and Nick still junked it up. Twenty half-eaten chicken boxes were in the fridge, along with about forty empty Hennessy and Grey Goose bottles. "Nick cut the beat down!" I said. "Come down, I gotta rap to you about something serious!"

In goofy Nick fashion he tripped down three steps in a size XXXX State Prop jumpsuit. It was green with fake inmate numbers on the front and back. "You see my wheels, nigga! I'ma fuck every girl eva, nigga!" he belted with a big wet Kool-Aid smile.

"We gotta talk, man," I said, pulling up a chair.

"What's wrong, Dee?"

"Yo, I'm done with Madeira Street. I'm sick of the shooting and Ike Guy and all that shit. You got two options. You can keep it and all the money from down there and work it by yourself or switch to this heroin wholesale shit with me and Troy. But I can't do that block shit anymore."

Nick looked at me like I lost my mind. "You dumb as shit if you walk away from all that money! Are you serious? A little beef make you leave that shit we built!"

"It's not just the beef. I'll hold my own, but I don't like being out there no more, plus I'm not chilling around here too much anymore," I said, surveying the trash. "I gotta tighten up. That block shit is stupid, I can't be workin' out of alleys, plus you gotta bunch crack in here. It smells like a kingpin charge in this bitch! I smelled that shit all the way across the street!"

"This ain't even you talkin'. Is it because of that girl, nigga!

She don't even know you!" screamed Nick. His jaws wiggled; he wiped his tears before they could spill.

"Naw, Nick, it's just time."

"Man, what the fuck ever, nigga!" he said, running back up the steps. "You fuckin' up, Dee. I don't know who you rappin' to, but you fuckin' all the way up!"

MADEIRA STREET

Man, am I gonna miss Madeira Street.

That block was hotter than fish grease in the summer and winter and I loved that. That made me. I speak up and out because of Madeira Street. Early on, that block showed me what it felt like to lose and bounce back.

I remember back in the day when this dude Kavon knocked me down in front of everybody. The whole hood laughed, even the girls I crushed on. He dug in my pockets and took my Lemonheads and Now and Laters, ate my snacks, kicked my ribs, called me a bitch and told me to go and get whoever I wanted because he'd do the same to them too. I ran home crying and told Bip. He loaded his gun with bullets and put extra ammo in his pockets, but I screamed, "No!"

Madeira Street taught me how to fight my own battles. That block showed me that the city made sidewalks because everybody didn't belong in the street.

I stayed away and heard that Kavon and those girls laughed for a week or so, but I knew I had to do something. I missed being out there and I knew I had to fight to get my name back.

I put a Master lock in a long Nike sock and came back around. Kavon was out like always with his head buried deep in a dice game. He screamed his point and snatched a couple dollars off of the curb; our eyes met and he laughed again. Everyone laughed—those same girls, even some of my homeboys joined in too.

He turned back around to gamble and I cracked him in the back of his head. Everybody jumped back. *Crack!* Hit his ass again, one to knock his fat ass out and another to wake fat ass up. *Crack!* One more to let his fat ass know that even though I don't look for trouble, I'll never turn it down.

We all got a little bloody that day and he definitely whipped my ass a few more times in the future but I didn't run anymore and he never went in my pockets again. Madeira Street challenged me to fight back and showed me the rewards of self-respect. I can hold my head up because of Madeira Street, which hurts because I can't really chill around there anymore.

I know that everybody's time on that block or any block eventually expires and my expiration date was right around the corner. Definitely too many murders around there and way too many incarcerations, all because dudes don't know when to leave the block alone. You gotta know when to let it go, and all of these signs were telling me that our time was done. I can't jug on blocks anymore. Selling drugs is about being mobile and switching up spots now.

I'll always be thankful for the valuable lessons, the sleepless nights, the bags of money, the ass whippings, the family I never knew I had, the family I will never forget, and everything else I gained and lost from that block.

Madeira Street made me a man. I can get through anything because of my time there.

TYLER REUNION

Nick needed a few weeks to cool off. The extra money he started making when I left Madeira Street made him forget about my presence in general—we even lost touch completely for a few days until he told me that he bumped into Tyler, the cool white boy I played ball with in college, at a gas station and gave him my number. Tyler buzzed my phone like crazy so I told him to meet me over Bethel Court, right at the tip of Douglass Housing Projects— pretty close to the basketball court where my cousin Damon was murdered back in the day. I posted up in the courtyard with Troy and Dog Boy while I waited. My .40-cal kept making my jeans sag so I grabbed a bigger jacket out of the car, the Burberry parka with the inside pocket.

About a half hour later, Tyler rolled up on us with Brad Pitt swag—he had on ripped-up jeans and a fitted leather.

"'Sup, fellas?" he said, taking a long drag of his Camel and plucking the butt as we all dapped him up.

"Why white people smoke Camels and black people smoke Newports, dug?" asked Dog Boy.

"It's racism, I tell you, racism!" I answered, looking at a chuckling Dog Boy. All fifty-six of his teeth showed every time he laughed. Tyler lit another. "Take a ride with me, white boy," I said, attempting to fix a stale blunt, trying to mend its cracked edges with saliva, nursing it back to health. My spit turned it into a noodle. I stuffed it behind my ear and I figured I could smoke it once it dried a little.

We pulled off in my car.

"So are you ever coming back to school? It's been like two fuckin' years!" he asked.

"Naw, man, fuck that school. Wanna grab a drink?"

"Always."

We weren't twenty-one; our bright eyes, tight skin, and naked faces gave us that preteen look. Our scraggly nonconnecting beards made it worse but my homie Fat Ivan from around the way was a bouncer at a little strip club on Baltimore Street so I drove there. A forty-dollar tip with a pound to Ivan, and Tyler and I slid through the front door to a mob of smoke, old heads, young dudes, and ass. Ass was everywhere. Big ass, tight ass, round asses with stretch marks or markless or muscle butts and those annoying triangle-shaped assess. They had flavors too, like high yellow, light skinned, brown skinned, dark skinned, and extra dark skinned, making up a rainbow coalition of equal-opportunity ass.

I spotted a chair at the end of the bar. "Can I smoke in here?" Tyler asked.

"Everybody else is, man! But look, you want to date a black girl? I can get you a date tonight! You ever been with a black girl?" I said, waving at the barmaid, Tonya. She looked at me and rolled her eyes.

"Not tonight, man, I wanted to talk to you about something else."

"Okay, Mr. Serious. Ah, gimme a Belvedere double with a li'l ice, what you want, Tyler?"

"I'll take a Corona." He chuckled. "Don't clown me, man!"

"Sixteen dollars, Mr. Too-Young-to-Drink, anything else?" said Tonya.

"Yeah, Mrs. Mind-Ya-Fuckin'-Business, get my man a Corona."

She laughed and rolled her eyes again.

Tonya used to live in my old building—drove niggas nuts back in the day. She's pudgy but you can still tell that she used to be built like one of those video chicks—all perfectly perky with a slim waist and a bubble butt. Now she has a three-baby-daddies gut, her edges are gone, and her face is all puffy from alcohol and stress. She was still kind of cute, though.

"Running to the rest room, bro!" said Tyler.

I nodded at him as I knocked my first drink back. Some other dudes from different parts of east Baltimore approached me as Tyler faded into the crowd like, "Who the fuck the white boy is? Fuck is up with you?"

I removed the blunt from my ear, lit it, and then hit it. Then I turned around, tilted my head, raised my eyebrow, and blew smoke at them before spinning back around on my barstool. My life, my family, and my street credentials were too intact for me to explain myself about anything to anyone ever. I been in the dope game and hailed from vets who never made statements and kept enough murderers around me for them to know not to ask me some stupid shit.

My second shot didn't stand a chance.

"Tonya, baby, gimmie another but make it a single!"

The bar was pitch dark and you couldn't really make out faces unless they were in kissing range. The girls were always different, well, the strippers at least, because Tonya was in there every time I was in there. Shit, she might've lived there. It also had upstairs that I never saw anyone use and cheesy Roman columns all over the place. About 90 percent of the women who worked there were down to fuck. Blowjobs were sixty-five dollars, protected sex was a hundred, and raw was one fifty.

Tyler came back. "Dee, so I came to talk to you about business, man. I want in. I can move that shit on campus," said Tyler.

I laughed. "One more and close me out!"

I wasn't laughing at Tyler's abilities and I'm sure that he was more than capable, but why? Why the fuck would he want to play this game?

"Dee, I'm telling you, I can make you a ton of fucking money!"

"This ain't the place. We'll rap."

DEE VERSUS TYLER

Tyler was born in an elite neighborhood full of homeowners, college graduates, and grass. His parks had benches and fountains and joggers and recycle bins. His doghouse had a doghouse and everyone had good credit. I'm from miles and miles and miles of concrete where everyone has fucked-up credit. Our credit is so fucked up, they won't take our cash. Our parks are concrete too—concrete open-air drug markets run by this crew or that crew—most of us have lead and some of us are crack babies and we all hoop, everyone hoops, even the grandmas.

Tyler played Little League baseball and his parents came to every game. They'd go out for pizza when he'd do well. They'd go out for pizza when he lost or for ice cream or his mom would make his favorite—casserole. He probably ate vegetables every day—ten-plus servings and went to bed by eight p.m. on school nights.

My hood didn't sleep, neither did I, and I never had vegetables as a kid—candy or carbs only, or noodles or cereal and I don't know what the fuck casserole is; I don't think black people eat it. My mom rarley attended any of my basketball games and I hated home-cooked meals before Angie's. My favorite dish as a kid was a chicken box with salt, pepper, and ketchup or a pack of Now and Laters or sixty-cent rice and gravy from Bo Bo's kitchen.

That restaurant was a death trap; it stayed wrapped up in caution tape—a lot of good dudes were murdered coming out of Bo Bo's.

In middle school Tyler came in second place in a science fair, he said. Supposedly he made a volcano that really erupted but lost to a kid who constructed some sort of remote control robot. He also said that he didn't give a shit about losing because he had baseball fame—enough fame to help him land his first kiss from a chick at a school dance.

I thought science fairs for were for the sitcoms I'd see it on TV. We'd always cut that shit off because the only experiment that mattered to us was transforming powder cocaine to hard crack rock. Well, not me, because I ain't hustle then, but the bulk of my friends did. I just rode dirt bikes up Ashland Avenue and past McElderey Street and on Jefferson Street, where I witnessed my cousin DI's murder and a few more bodies dropped after that. I lost my virginity in between those funerals. Being horny kept me indoors when them shots rang out and probably saved my life.

Tyler went to one of those elite boarding schools. It sat in the middle of green acres under clear skies. He lived on a campus that was equipped with horse stables and tennis courts and where the girls were separated from the boys. They had lunch options and a salad bar and bottled water way back in the nineties before people started drinking bottled water. They read the classics like Shakespeare and Hemingway and had rich discussions centered around art, history, and modern culture. Tyler said his schools were 99.9 percent nonviolent and I replied, "Ninety-nine point nine percent?" He then told me that one time a kid had brought a knife to his school, showed it, was snitched on by everyone who saw it, and then was quickly apprehended. No one was hurt.

Sometimes I'd forget my jacket or my science book, but I never left my pistol—that .22 fit right in the inside pocket of my Pelle. By sixteen I lost a bunch of good friends to murder, and I didn't want to join the club. We used to bump our old school classics like NWA, Black Moon, and Smith and Wesson on portable CD players and no one I knew read shit ever. The girls mixed with the boys way too much. Everybody fucked everybody raw. First period smelled like STDs. Other than daily fistfights and a few stabbings, my school wasn't the most violent inside but we were surrounded by five rival housing projects. I had family in them all and still got banked once or twice.

Tyler was successfully finishing semester after semester of college. I dropped out. Tyler has never been to prison and is 100 percent employable. I never been to prison and felt 100 percent unemployable. Tyler's dad has a business that he could work for even though his mom told him that he didn't have to work unless he wanted to. I gotta work, no one will give me shit. Tyler got some job offers from some family friends as well but respectfully declined. I put in a bunch of applications and didn't get a callback. We both smoke and drink. Tyler's room, board, and car are all pre-paid by family so him not making any money today really didn't matter. I have a hungry crew to feed, rent and a Nike addiction so I'm happy as shit that Troy and I have weight and a nice clientele. I wasn't sure if Tyler wanted to make his own money or was just infatuated with the life like everyone else, but I told him I'd think on it.

TYLER'S BLOCK

I decided to let Tyler get down. The rich white money looked good to me. Plus he was smart, a quick learner, and I could just tax him enough so I could make the same amount of money while lightening my workload.

I had been away from Madeira Street for like two months and I didn't really miss it. Not even a little. Soni and I were joined at the hip now. If you saw her, then you saw me. I even talked her into moving into the Green House with me by basically promising her that I wouldn't be in the streets anymore and I wasn't—because I hustled weight out of my car now.

Soni and I were creating an amazing life—like made-for-TV. She decorated the hell out of our apartment with white couches, futuristic glass tables, and African artwork. We went to the farmers market and bought fresh vegetables that tasted delicious. She introduced me to organic markets where everything cost a hundred dollars, even the 99-cent bottled waters, but most important, I started reading some of her African American history books.

I already knew about our history as revolutionaries from the stuff my brother taught me, but her books opened me up to all types of black history on a level deeper than my original understanding. The stuff my grade school teachers left out. I never knew that African Americans accomplished so many amazing things in science, art, and literature. I began to develop a greater understanding that stretched far beyond drugs, junkies, and the bubble I was in.

Part of me knew that Soni knew I was hustling because only drug dealers and the top 1 percent of Americans can afford to push a cart through Whole Foods like we did—we filled it up with organic everything from our eggs to our trash bags made out of environmentally friendly plastic. Drugs paid our expensive bills, and my taste for luxury was starting to rub off on her a little. She also got used to the idea of what I was doing. It didn't bother her because I didn't talk about it, plus I was so smooth, seamless even, it was almost like I didn't hustle.

Most of my days were free. I'd see Old Head like twice for simple conversations that mainly consisted of him giving me game on life and my health. He loved that I lived downtown, stayed away from the block and what I told him about Soni and me. "Have kids! Life is about having kids!" he'd tell me every time, right before I left. Troy and I picked up drugs from his workers biweekly and from there we'd bust the bricks down into ounces and grams and then distribute.

I had clients all over the city who were always ready. Great clients who I'd front if their money was funny or if they had faced some sort of loss. There was never any hassle or beef because there was no block for me to fight over. My dope was great. I was always on time and I stayed under the radar. Soni and I talked about me going back to college every day and I started looking at schools and some different programs. I knew I didn't want to go back to

Loyola, but I did want to stay in Baltimore. I also wanted to start a business like Old Head said.

Troy and I had previously been talking about buying a liquor store but now he just sold dope and fucked—all day every day. I couldn't even get him on the phone anymore unless it was business related—but the game does that.

BIRTHDAY BRAWL

Yo, Dee, you can't say no! We goin' out tonight! And you can't say no! We need to celebrate!" screamed Nick, leaping his whale of a self on my back. It was his birthday and he had been popping Perks and drinking since I came by to drop his gift off, a stainless steel Rolex with the date—just identical to the one Hurk had bought me way back when he started hustling. Nick tore it out the pack and put it on his right arm.

"Yo, Breitling on my left and Rollie on my right, we goin' out tonight!" he said, dancing like Puff Daddy all around the kitchen.

"You a fat clown!" Long Tooth yelled from the steps.

Everybody was over at Angie's. She made a huge down-south type of breakfast with fried eggs, fried bacon, fried catfish, fried pancakes, and fried everything else—I think she tried to fry the orange juice.

"Yo, you don't pop pills no more! You don't come out no more! What's up!" yelled Nick. His eyes were redder than strawberries. I couldn't even see his pupils. His teeth looked rotten and fragile too. The more I hung with Soni, the less I drank, but seeing him made me want to quit that too. I probably used to look like him.

"Fuck you, Nick, because you ugly, I'm gonna go out! I know you won't get no girls if I'm not there so I'm gonna go out for you, fat boy!" I said.

Angie made me a big plate. Two bites and I wanted to toss it. I looked around and saw everyone else swallowing whole plates. Dog Boy didn't even stop to breathe, Nick had seconds and thirds, Long Tooth flossed with a pig spine, and some of the new kids ate like they never had a plate before.

"You need a mug fuckin' restaurant Miss Angie!" some girl yelled while tonguing a catfish tail, making sure no meat was left. That food tasted like grease with diabetes sprinkled on top. I can't believe I used to eat that every day. Angie used to feed me and before her I ate nothing but fried crab cake dinners or cups of noodles. I would've probably been dead if I didn't hoop so much.

"I feel sick, somebody want my plate?" The whole entire house leaped over me, gold teeth hit me from every direction—my food disappeared in seconds. My plate was licked clean, shined with saliva and placed back in front of me.

"You too good for my cookin' now! You gotta cute li'l girlfriend and now y'all eat fancy!" said Miss Angie, wrapping her huge fluffy arms around me.

"Yes, Miss Angie, I am too good," I replied with a straight face. Then she tickled me until I couldn't hold my laugh anymore. I promised to take her shopping at a healthy market; I couldn't have Miss Angie OD'ing on salt, fat, and processed crap.

"Yo, I'll see the rest of y'all bums at the club!" I said, trading handshakes with everyone and a big hug with Angie.

Later that day I was getting dressed for Nick's party. Gucci sweater, Gucci belt, and Prada sneakers—basically my wholesaler uniform. Soni snuck up and wrapped her arms around me while I checked myself out in the mirror.

"You be safe with those thugs, okay! I'm so scared! You too cute to be around them anyway."

I spun around and kissed her forehead. "I'm chilling for like a hour or two. I'll see you later, babe," I said, pecking her forehead again.

"I love you!"

"Love you too!"

I pulled up in front of the club and parked by a fire hydrant. The line rapped around the side of the building. Dudes in sweaters and Aldo shivering next to girls in shinny-skimpy skirts and high heels. I knew the bouncers and the promoters, which meant a bunch of things, like I didn't have to freeze on line. I didn't get patted down. I didn't pay to get in and we already had a couple of tables. I was one of the last from my crew to arrive. Nick stood on the couch wearing the two watches with a bottle of champagne in each hand. He had another tucked in the back pocket of his jeans. Dog Boy nodded in a stupor, LT nudged me when I reached our section and said Dog Boy had been asleep in there all night. The place was packed with thugs and model types. They girls were pretty but they weren't Soni. Nick leaped off of the couch when he saw me. "Yo, you gotta meet Ronny, my nig!"

Ronny was Nick's new connect, a forty-something wild Jamaican with big sleepy eyes and balding dreads. I didn't know him well, but I heard he chopped a guy's head off down Lafayette back in ninety-something. Who knows if it was true or not, but his clout was real and he'd probably kill Nick if he messed up his money.

"Ronnie, this Dee, man, he my bro." Nick grabbed us both. "We all gotta link, man, this real family shit!"

Ronnie extended his hand. "Me hear you 'bout your business. We should rap soon, brudda."

I gave him a firm shake. "No doubt, Dread."

The club thickened, other crews showed up; east Baltimore was everywhere with some cool dudes from west and couple of Cherry Hill cats. We were packed in, sideways walking and squeeze-through room only. I was trying to push through to get Dog Boy so we could slide. I reached the VIP section and said, "Yo, let's blow this spot! It's too hot in here!"

"Loooooooooooook, Dee!" he said, pointing to the other side of the club.

Nick was fussing with a dude. I fought through the crowd and got close enough to see Nick hit the dude in the head with a Cristal bottle. The dude's knees buckled and hit the floor. Another guy picked him up before he fell and held his limp body up. Nick woke him up with two more blows across his face and then put him to sleep with an upper cut. The kid looked finished but east Baltimore wasn't. A collage of every block and crew from my side of town united on this guy's head. I pulled Nick away from the melee. Timberland boots, Nike Air Force 1s, flowerpots, pint glasses, and everything else crushed his body. It was a modern lynching. His complexion was blood; I wasn't sure if he was dead or not but I bet he wished he was. They brought his limp body out on a stretcher. It took me and Dog Boy to drag Nick to the car. Everyone cheered at the body. I wondered where his friends were. And if he was dead, who would be charged with the murder? What in the fuck was wrong with those guys? What in the fuck was wrong with me?

"Yo, nigga, let's hit Norma's!" screamed a half-drunk Nick, pulling away. I locked on his drunk body and flung us to the ground. He popped up before me and dropped his gun. Dog Boy grabbed it. "You actin' dumb, bitch! Chill!" he yelled, tucking the gun in his dip. The whole police department was on Eutaw now, right in front of the club. I hit the automatic start on my car. "Come on, man, we gotta roll!" Nick was squatting in the alley shitting. Dog Boy approached him and he spit some red and green shit right in his direction.

"I'm not gonna leave ya fat ass—come on!" Dog Boy yelled at Nick, trying not to step in the shit or the throw-up on the sidewalk. Nick headlocked Dog Boy and they circled. "You wannnn fight boy, come on! You think you grown?"

I jumped back out of the car and threw a wide haymaker at Nick's jaw: one blow stretched him out. His own pile of shit and throw-up broke his fall. We dragged his fat body to the back of my car.

"Never again!" I yelled. "Yo really smell like shit in my car! I just got this detailed!"

"What you wanted to leave him, Dee! Damn, he drunk!" said Dog Boy, rubbing his neck.

"Fuck you. I'm taking my girl and her mom to the movies tomorrow! They don't wanna smell this shit! I don't wanna smell this shit!"

Dog Boy tried to say I was overreacting. I turned the music up over whatever he was talking about. I hoped that kid didn't die. Everybody knows Nick; what if they finger him? Everybody knows us; what if it's me? One drunk night could ruin everything. And I wasn't even drunk.

THE OTHER BALTIMORE

Dude, you ever heard of Radiohead?" asked Tyler, pushing in a CD and enhancing the volume.

"Naw, I only listen to rappers and R & B singers who dress like rappers," I replied.

Dog Boy laughed and said, "Dat's real shit, bro bro! Real shit!"

"Tylerrrr, why you do this? Like ain't you rich or something?" Dog Boy asked from the backseat.

Dog Boy had a beef with some dudes from the Jefferson side of Madeira Street. They shot at him twice and he put some gun work in too. I kept feeding him money and tried to keep him around me until it cooled off but he was eager to get back out there.

"Because this is America, Dog Boy, and Americans are responsible for making money all of the time," Tyler replied.

Tyler was a natural. He was never short and didn't know how to make excuses or complain. I used to roll with him sometimes when he made his drop-offs to stressed Hopkins kids, skinny art students, and the church boys at Loyola who liked to party. He was really smooth too. We'd stop at a bar, he'd introduce me as a college buddy, and then exchange a shake where he'd extend a hand full of work and draw back a fist full of cash—done. Tyler didn't come out for anything under five grams, never gave credit, and he didn't need to, because his clients had money and privilege.

They weren't like mine. Tyler and I always joked about how if he and a customer got caught in the middle of a transaction, they'd be diagnosed as junkies and sent to rehab, but the same cop could catch me and I would be headed to jail for the rest of my life on kingpin charges. Dog Boy and I were taking wild risk in a world that gave Tyler zero consequences, and we both knew it all boiled down to one thing—skin color.

Tyler's sales were all in bars, shops, and restaurants that I'd never been to. Colorful places full of hip patrons with black-framed specs and vintage leathers. I learned about six nice food spots that I took Soni to just by making drop-offs with him. Chilling around Tyler showed me a side of Baltimore that I didn't know existed.

It also showed me how segregated Baltimore really was. I grew up in a neighborhood where everyone was black except for the liberal teachers and housing police. Our city could basically be split up in to two categories—black and white.

The Black Baltimore was all about Grey Goose vodka, Hennessy and Pepsi, crack sales, making money and running to the outskirts of the city, playing basketball, paying forty dollars to get into parties with fifteen-dollar drinks, cookouts, corner stores, being harassed by cops, pit bulls, dirt bikes, church, and staying in black areas.

White Baltimore, which in most cases is only two miles away from these black areas, is all about Ketel One or Stoli vodka, Jack Daniel's whiskey and Coke, sniffing coke, labradors, eating outside, free entrance into clubs where you buy one drink and get another free, barbecues, free-range chickens, playing Frisbee, jogging, being loved by cops, and staying in white areas.

The only things that connected the city were the Ravens and me and Tyler getting all that dope money from both sides.

Tyler was also doing well in school. He had multiple exit strategies, ways to flip all of the money he made into something legal. He always talked about investing, traveling the world after he graduated, and then coming back to start a business in L.A. or someplace warm.

"Dude, are you going to *Scarface* it to the bloody end?" he asked me one day.

I didn't really have a plan but real estate seemed easy—buy a property, rent it out, stack the money, and sell it.

Tyler's parents lived in Roland Park, an elite area of the city, but they also owned the brownstone in Bolton Hill that he lived in. It was split up into four units. He lived in one and they rented out the rest. I loved that neighborhood and thought I could probably do the same. I had a bunch of cash put up, and being the Donald Trump of the ghetto seemed like a pretty prestigious gig.

1046 WEST LOMBARD

A pack of nurses surrounded Mr. Pete. He was trash talking as usual with that sideways smile. They giggled like schoolgirls as he hit them with a joke after a compliment followed by another joke. I admired from a distance until he spotted me.

"Young boy, get over here!"

I stepped to him; the nurses took a walk so that we could handle our business.

"I'm taking your advice, Mr. Pete, and starting a business!"

"Tell me something good, young blood," Mr. Pete replied, sitting up in his chair, fully alert, proud and anxious.

"I'm gonna buy one of those apartment house joints and rent the units out, like a Donald Trump type."

Mr. Pete told me to never call myself Donald Trump because Donald Trump is a dumbass. He said that Trump was born into money so his success was guaranteed, whereas I'm from the gutter so I'm expected to stay. He then said Trump's casino went bankrupt.

"How a casino go bankrupt? That's the only business where people just give you their money, right?" I asked.

"Cuz he's a dumbass! I just told you that, pay attention! You a young black genius. Poisoned by many buckets of lead paint but still a genius, don't forget that!"

Mr. Pete then told me that real estate was the move. He said America is all about owning land.

"You'll always be treated as a second-class citizen until you own some land, boy, and as you can see, I'm a first-class nigga!"

I'm a sponge around Mr. Pete, I just absorb game.

"Get a real estate agent, boy, and check out this li'l bar on Lombard Street by Hollis Market. A lady named Lonnie own and I heard it's for sale. That would be a great way for you to enter the game!"

"I'm on it."

I was all gassed when I left the clinic and hit Soni up to tell her the news.

Ring ring ring...

"Hey, Dee, wassup."

"Baby, you know a real estate agent? Mr. Pete put me on to this bar on Lombard Street and I'm going to buy it!"

"Wow, Dee, wow. That's just what the black community needs, another liquor store!"

"Naw, because mine will be different. It will be black-owned, black-operated, and I'll be giving out black jobs to black ass people, so chill your black ass out!"

Soni laughed. "I'll text you the number to my aunt's agent and a list of things I need from Whole Foods. Bye!" Whole Foods. Whole Foods was the reason I needed to keep making money with their twenty different types of apples that all cost five dollars apiece and had exotic names like brands of weed.

I called the agent, left a message, and headed to the market. She didn't call by the time I was finished grocery shopping, so I drove over to the property.

The bar Mr. Pete directed me to was set in between two other bars but that didn't bother me. Streets taught me how to deal with competition. The awning was dated and dusty. It read "Stadium Hideaway" in big crusty black letters. A few tough guys and some heroin addicts lingered around the front and up and down the side street. I walked past them and went in. Bulletproof glass and forty-ounce posters were everywhere. There was another door covered with black tint. I pulled the handle. A middle-aged, light-skinned woman cracked the door. "The lounge is closed, baby, but you can buy some drink to go, though." I told her I was good and stepped. The agent called me back and introduced herself. Her phone voice exploded through my receiver: "Hello, Dee! I'm Joan!"

She said that we could check the place out tomorrow. I said I saw enough and I wanted to own it.

"We can definitely put in an offer, Dee!" she yelled. I had to pull my cell away from my ear. She told me that the place was $150K and asked me if I had a loan. I really had enough cash to buy the place outright, but I thought I'd inquire about a home loan so that I could build some credit. Pete said I needed credit.

"Call my mortgage broker. Her name is Sherry Lass. I'll shoot you her info!"

I knew it was after hours and most offices would be closed but I called Sherry and left a message on the voice mail because I wanted to be the first person she heard in the a.m. My heart pumped. This felt right, maybe the first right thing I felt since the first time I met Soni.

NO DOC ZONE

Sherry Lass called me at nine a.m. sharp the next morning sounding like she just downed a gallon of espresso—asking for my FICO score and for pay stubs and what type of down payment I had. I swear all of these middle-aged businesswomen suck on bottles of energy all day. I told her I didn't have anything but a bunch of cash my grandparents left me in their will, which was a super lie, but I guess she bought it because she invited me up to her office out White Marsh, which was about a twenty-minute drive from the city.

I gave her my Social Security number over the phone and Joan had sent her the property info so I fried an egg and headed her way. Her office was in a park of offices that looked like a housing projects for businesses. Take away the logos on the doors and every space would be identical. Her spot was called United Capital Mortgage Brokers.

"You must be Dee!" she said when I walked through the door. Sherry was a pint-sized white woman who could fit in my pocket— she wore a blazer, a brooch, and a pack of thin gold chains. Her hair was blond and she seemed to be in a rush, a familiar rush. The kind of the rush I liked—the kind that only comes with that hustler's spirit.

"Your credit isn't great but it isn't bad, hon; I've seen worse.

Question, you have an unpaid Macy's account from 1993. How did you have a Macy's account in 1993? Weren't you like a baby?"

"I don't know, can you fix it?" I asked.

"Sure, Dee, now where do you work and how much can you put down?"

I told her that I didn't have a job, and that's why I was starting a business. She left the room, huddled up with some of her coworkers and came back.

"Dee, we are mortgage brokers, not a bank. That means we have relationships with hundreds of banks that offer all types of nontraditional loans. You qualify for a no doc loan."

"No doc loan?" I said. "What's that?"

"Well, Dee, it's a special loan for people who don't really have a job or credit. The fees are higher but I can get you into that property." She got up and closed the door. "Now the other option is me getting you some pay stubs and tax records from a friend. That costs a little but it can be done. What do you choose?"

My brain told me to get away from this lady—her plan sounded like a federal indictment waiting to happen—but my gut said she was cool and instinct had brought me that far, so I said, "The no doc loan sounds cool. Let's do it."

"The rate is going to be a little high but pay the mortgage on time and I'll refinance you in a year. Now it's going to be about seventy-five thousand dollars down, and the liquor license comes with the store. Can you swing that?"

"Yeah. Should I go grab it now?"

"No, Dee." She laughed. "You don't need it until settlement! I'm going to like working with you, hon!"

MURDERLAND

Get up and get your phone, Dee! Long Face or Teeth or whatever that boy name is keep calling!" Soni yelled, digging my cell into my chest.

I woke up, grabbed my phone, and dialed him back. "Dee, we out front, come out." I love my friends because they are my friends, but I hate them for that reason too. Who pops up in front of your crib and calls until you come out? Really. I threw on a sweat suit and headed out to meet the goons. Most of the people in my building were young and white. They never said hello, they just looked at me with tight smiles. I was raised to only speak to people who speak to me. I ignored everyone in the building because they ignored me, and it was pretty peaceful.

My homies posted up directly in front of my building in a black Jeep that I never saw before. I knew these were my friends because the windows were pitch black but cracked—weed clouds floated out. There was no tag on the front of the car.

I hopped in the back.

"Yoooooooooo, what's up, bro!" screamed Mac. Long Tooth pulled off. Hurk removed his hood and peeked around from the passenger seat. "Surprise, nigga!" He laughed. "Dee, Mac wanted to see you first—he fresh outta Jessup and ready to put that work in!"

Mac was Hurk's cousin and the real life O-Dog from *Menace II*

Society—America's worst nightmare: young, black, and just didn't give a fuck. A real shoot-first, ask-questions-later type, nice with his hands, and known for knife work too. A few years back a group of dudes in white tees sprayed champagne all over the club—some hit our section. Mac whipped out a six-inch blade and turned all of their t-shirts red. I remember the whole section staggering and dripping out of the main entrance while Mac laughed hysterically, cleaning the knife on his denims.

"Man, you need a nigga hit, call me, we get rey lock this whole town on some Anthony Jones shit, nigga!" screamed Mac, spilling his Tanqueray on the Glock planted in his lap.

"Man, y'all dudes hot as shit! Riding around with dark-ass tints, guns and no front tag! Drop me back off!" I laughed.

Long Tooth circled the block and said, "Lemme ride down the jets real quick and grab some money, we can hop in your car and head out the mall. It's new dope dealers out!" I definitely agreed.

On the ride down, Hurk told me that he shot at some dudes that was talking shit about us last night and needed ten thousand dollars from me so that he could hide down south for a minute. I'm pretty sure no one said anything about me because I hadn't even been outside, but I couldn't wait to give him the money just so he could go away. That $10K could potentially put him and his BS out of my life forever. He wasn't my brother anymore, and definitely didn't care about my well-being—I couldn't wait to buy him out of my life. Me, Troy, and Tyler had a nice safe thing going and I didn't want to mess that up.

Long Tooth was looking down at his phone and almost hit a dude on Caroline Street. He swerved just in time to get around him. We saw him yell something with his arms up in the rearview.

"Yo! Stop the car!" Mac yelled. Long Tooth slammed on the

brakes. Mac popped out the back door and threw four shots at the guy and then jumped back in.

"Yo! I'm not playin' wit' anybody!" he yelled, squeezing the smoking pistol. The rest of the car laughed. These dudes could definitely get me killed within hours. I sat in silence and didn't really say much of anything until we reached the projects.

"Yo, LT, buy me the tennis and I'll pay you back. Hurk, you can get the money from Dog Boy and I'll check y'all later, I'ma kick down here for a while. Welcome home, Mac," I said before strolling over to the court. I took a few jump shots with some skinny kids. They called me crazy and phony for not riding out with them. I waved them off and stopped to watch the Jeep pull away. They'll probably die or catch a thousand years today, I thought as I started a game of fifty. That bar is going to save me.

CODED

Lass called me up and said the deal went through. I just had to come to her office and sign some papers. Joan would also be there, so I would get a chance to meet her too. I had to go and see Mr. Pete. I knew he would be proud. He kept talking about throwing a party for me on my opening night. All the nurses said they were coming in their Coach and Dooney & Bourke. I was like, "Naw, those brands are wack! My people rock Gucci and Loui V!"

I pulled up to the unit with some pictures of the property that I yanked off of the Internet. I had been carrying them around everywhere since I first looked that the store. I couldn't stop looking at them and envisioning myself as the boss of the store, slapping high-fives and pouring shots.

An ugly silence hit me when I walked into the unit. A few nurses lingered by the entrance.

"Hey, Kim, Pete get here yet?" I asked.

"Oh, I'm so sorry, baby, he coded and had been taken out earlier," she said, giving me a big hug.

"Okay, well, I'll see y'all next time."

"Really? You're still gonna come here?"

"Of course!" I told her, Pete's my OG. Why wouldn't I? She asked to rap to me but I didn't have time for small talk. I had just picked up a lot of dope from his worker a few days ago and it had to be bussed down. Getting off the block was the best thing that has ever happened to me. Even with all the Hurk stuff going on, not being on the block had just made me feel safe.

Pete taught me how to think. How to analyze the system and everyone it affects on top of why cops respond the way they do. He told me that the police department and prison system are just an extension of slavery and the cops are the slave catchers. He said America runs on criminal justice and they use us dudes to sell smack so that the country can run. I never left him without a lesson; he's a walking bookshelf, the Internet before the Internet. He'd say: "Dee, why do you think the dude who steals fifty million dollars in a white-collar scandal gets eighteen months in prison while the dude who robs a bar with a gun for three hundred dollars gets thirty years! Because the white-collar guy is going for a sting—he'll never have to steal again—while the guy with the gun will probably have to pull a job later that day!" I got game from him and then gave it to my young boys.

I called Troy to tell him that Pete coded and about my store. He was still too busy to answer my calls so I hit him two more times. He picked up.

"Yo, what's good, bro?" I said.

"Nothing, man. I'm fucked up over Pete, man, that shit hurt!"

"Yeah, I just left the clinic, I heard he coded but we'll see him when he back, bro. Chill out. We got work to do!"

"Dee, coded means dead. You code and they can save you, but sometimes you die. Mr. Pete is dead and he ain't coming back!"

I pulled over and stepped out of the car. My stomach boiled, my chest crumbled. I bent over and I threw up brown shit all over the curb and my sneakers. A slide show of his life played in my head. I could see him as a young G on the avenue, leaning on his big

Caddy, counting money in front of his club, not making a living but making a killing like he always said. I could see his smile and that vision put the brakes on my anxiety.

Dude was a legend, and I was happy to know him. It's gonna take awhile to get over this one. RIP, Mr. Pete.

THE NEW OWNER

Lass recommended that I wear a tie to my first settlement. She said it was good luck. I decided to go with sweatpants and an Air Jordan tee. Troy went to Mr. Pete's funeral a day before but I skipped it. He was a great guy, but I just felt like that was something for his real family. I wanted to be there, but instead I viewed his body and sent flowers.

Joan met me at the title company. She rolled in looking like the mom from *The Sopranos* with a fur jacket and two ringing cells. She was a walking call center.

"Hey, nice to meet you finally—you are a cutie and so young. What are you, fourteen?" I laughed.

Buying this property was everything to me. I knew Mr. Pete was smiling down on me from heaven or cheering me on from hell. Either way, he taught me that America is about ownership and I was finally joining the club.

The dude at the title company said that the owners had already signed their papers and all I had to do was sign the same docs and drop off the down payment which ended being $67,000. Giving myself a small business loan was a great feeling. I brought cash to the table—some fifties and hundreds. My agent shrugged and the title guy looked at me like I was crazy. "You know, Dee, people usually bring us certified checks from the banks they do business with!"

"Okay, I'll do that the next time."

I signed papers until my arm was sore. They gave me the keys and I did it. I owned my first piece of land. I couldn't wait to have a grand opening with all of my family and friends—even though I bought the spot, I planned on it being a place for everyone. I told Troy to meet me at my bar. He was hitting me all day and I knew why. Mr. Pete is gone now and he wanted a backup plan, just in case the connection stopped.

The bar looked good on the inside. It was a little dirty and tacky for my taste, but that was an easy fix—other than that, it was fully stocked and everything worked. The inside was a little tighter than I remembered, and three huge poker machines had clogged the pathway. I thought I could move them and create some space for people to dance.

I walked up the stairs to see the two units advertised in the listing—apartments over the bar that I could rent out for around six hundred dollars apiece, which would cover the mortgage. They were stinky and shabby but again, nothing that a dope fiend cleaning crew couldn't fix. This business stuff seemed almost too easy. Buy low, sell high.

Troy pulled up.

"This look good, bro!" he yelled. "I'm proud of you, man!"

"Come on, bro, check the inside out!" I told him.

We sat at the counter and I poured us two big cups of Absolut. Troy began telling me about Pete's funeral and how OG's in Lincolns and big Caddy's were all over the place. He said that beautiful women stretched across the room and he felt's Pete's spirit gracing the crowd.

"Damn bro I should've went."

"On another note Dee, if we don't have a connect, I'm taking this half of brick to the block to buy some time."

"Chill, man, I'll find you a connect. Relax; don't you have some money saved?"

He tilted his head. "Yo, I'm flat broke, man. All I got is these drugs, shit, I ain't know Pete was gonna die. I been fuckin' money up, and what you mean find me a connect?"

"Yo, I'm out. I don't sell drugs anymore. I'm done!"

Troy laughed and paused. "Are you serious?" he said, standing up. "And what the fuck I'm post to do, nigga!"

"Well, one, you gonna calm the fuck down! You gotta half a brick of heroin, that's more than enough to be straight. Stop feeding them girls and buying those silly clothes. I'll find you a connect, but I'm done, man. I ain't plan on doing this forever!" I climbed on the countertop and held my red cup into the air. "I'm done!"

I felt like I won—like the American Dream was really happening for me. My family has been here for hundreds of years; however, I was the first real American citizen because I owned a store, could create jobs, was with a woman who was finishing college, and I could go to college if I wanted to or buy more land. I have credit, I'm legal, and I'll never go to jail.

I made it.

Good-bye to the game.

Even though I said wouldn't hustle forever, a huge part of me thought I'd do this drug shit forever. Probably because you were the only game I knew. Not just me, black kids everywhere. Ain't no STEM around here, all we learn is you and hoops. And if you know like I know, everybody can't hoop.

I thought I'd hustle, pitch, trap, get rid of, jug, sell, move and slang drugs forever. I got in with the intention of making a lot of money. And I did. I got that.

I got that. I got real estate, I got a bar. I also got jackers watching, I got enemies, I got shot at, I got a new gun, I got dead friends, I got demons, I got dependents, I got stress, I got funeral bills, I got happy customers, I got bails, I got bills, I got mad customers, I got a drinking problem, I beat a Perk problem but I got problems, I got real problems.

I got people that count on me being a criminal and I have to let them down because I got reasons to live, and playing this game only guarantees death.

But I'll always remember that dope-boy feeling. Buying that chain in the display case, pulling that new Benz off the lot, hooping in brand new two-hundred-dollar sneakers and giving them away, just giving shit away for the sake of giving shit away—giving money away, giving money to people who needed it and to people that don't. Living.

Being the car show, the fashion show, and the provider, the guy you could get tuition or a small business loan from. The center of my community. Some of those preachers never gave back, they parked Benzes in the hood and never gave back, but us, the dope boys—we gave back. Jobs, money, and opportunity: the only company that always hires felons.

I'm gonna miss that dope-boy feeling, that sharp fade, those new sweats, and those two phones with no space in my voice mail because everybody reached out all of the time.

What a feeling, but I'm sure I'll have new experiences. I'm gonna fly straight and push for a real life. I ain't never coming back.

Peace,

Dee

P.S. I'm leaving my trap-phone to Troy. That little Nokia is a goldmine. Sales call it all day and all night so he'll be great. One Love.

HEALTH CARE

I was down Angie's waiting for Dog Boy to meet me so I could set up something with him and Troy. I dozed on her plastic chair covers till Joan called me up to tell me how Soni was going to love the Viking stove that came with the place she had just found me, because it could bake a whole turkey in an hour. "Wow! I wonder how long would it take to make a grilled cheese?" I asked.

Joan and I had a real working relationship. She sold me two properties in a month—the bar, a rental on Belair Road, and now we are working on my castle, a home in Bolton Hill, but not like Tyler's family. I want all three or four thousand square feet to myself—a Cosby-like brownstone with modern features.

"Okay, Joan, take Soni to see it and if she likes it, draw up the contract."

Dog Boy spilled through the door leaking. His red drippy hands wrapped his own torso as he fell toward me. He collapsed with bug eyes before tilting his head toward heaven. Miss Angie saw the blood from the top of the steps.

"Oh God, oh God, oh God!" she screamed like a lottery winner. Cops, ambulance. I'm calling them," Miss Angie said, trembling. I grabbed both of her meaty arms.

"Calm down, Angie, get some towels and water. Don't call anyone!"

We never call police unless we need reports for insurance purposes. Hero cops are fictional like Santa Claus and affirmative action. Plus we were on Madeira Street—pizza guys and cops never come when you call.

"What should I do with these towels?"

"Throw them over the blood!" I replied. Dog Boy moaned and rocked on his side. I told him to stay still.

"Done, what do you want me to do with this water?" said Miss Angie—still shaking. I didn't even know why I told her to get water; it just sounded right.

"Sit here with Dog Boy while I go get Disco. Don't open the door for anyone, he'll be okay." I sprung out of the front door and hopped off the steps. Nick waited at the bottom.

"Go back in the house, boy, I was coming in. Them niggas that shot Dog Boy circled the block!" said Nick as he pulled me down low to the ground. I got on all fours and leaned my back against someone's car.

Nick looked horrible—like a functioning junkie—and he smelled like shit. Those Perks had him all messed up. His skin was soggy, he scratched until blood surfaced, and his eyes were piss-colored.

"Yo, I gotta go and get Disco. Dog Boy's bleeding like a muthafucka!" I said, peeking up to see if the coast was clear. "Who shot him? Who he beefin' with now?"

"You wouldn't believe me. Dog Boy slapped some nigga and he came around here three or four times today bangin' guns like Rambo. Take this and go back in the house. I'll get Disco," replied

Nick as he handed me a .45. It was black, gray, two-toned, and cocked.

Dog Boy had the living room smelling like baked scabs. Miss Angie said the bullet went through the right side of his chest. This was the first time I ever saw him speechless. It hurt because I was powerless. I kneeled down and scooped the back of his head with my palm. "Miss Angie, get me another cold washcloth! I gotta clean him up; you'll be okay, Dog Boy. Stay with me." I had to make sure he stayed still because I didn't know if a bullet was still in him. Angie could've been wrong. Moving a body with a bullet in it could cause it to pop around and hit a vital organ or something. Nick and Disco were taking forever. I had to talk to Dog Boy. I thought talking would calm him—it definitely calmed me. I joked about his speech impediment. I rubbed the cloth across his temple and reminded him of the house raid when Fat Tay dumbass tried to flush a small pistol down the toilet. I reminded him of the time he fucked Liz with the peg leg and then stole it for proof and how we used to ride our dirt bikes through Pat's kitchen, do doughnuts in her living room and then wheelie out the front door.

Miss Angie said Disco was outside. "Yo, let her in!" I yelled. Disco walked in with a multicolor windbreaker on with two-strapped Reeboks and a glittery bag to match. She looked like a pack of Life Savers.

"Gib him a pill for da pain. Dis ain't shit but a hole, baby!" said Disco, lighting a Newport and analyzing the wound. I didn't have any strong prescription pills, but there was a bottle of Motrin, so she spoon-fed him that. Dog Boy had the same drug tolerance as some of these fiends he served—too high to catch a buzz off of ibuprofen, but something was better than nothing.

Disco dipped into her bag and started dabbing the hole with

rubbing alcohol–soaked gauze. Dog Boy squeezed my hand, making my complexion as red as the blood on his damp tee. Miss Angie prayed to Jesus.

Disco started sewing his skin like fabric. She wove the needle in and out in perfect equal stitches. Dog Boy quailed with every poke but got used to it as she started on his back. I interrupted Miss Angie's prayer and told her to call around for some pain pills. Her tears were enough to wash the blood off of the floor—I could've put a "Wet Floor" sign down.

"Take my belt off, Yo. Don't let shit hit my belt. I love you, Disco, but you ugly as shit!" mumbled Dog Boy. Disco laughed and patted the back of his head. I unlatched his black Damier belt. The LV buckle weighed at least a pound, I thought as I pulled it off. I wiped the belt down with tap water, dried it, and rolled it up like it was new. Miss Angie ran in the kitchen and told me that LT had a line on some Oxys for Dog Boy's pain.

"So Dog Boy is stable?" she asked.

"Yeah, he's gonna be okay," I replied.

"You're not going to do anything crazy, are you?"

Twenty minutes later I got up with Mac, Long Tooth, and Nick. We strapped up with heavy artillery and loaded up in the Camry. My family sedan was a tank with choppers, handguns, extended clips, and cartons of bullets. I blasted the radio to shake Nick out of his nod.

"Yo, you rockin' on a mission, that's crazy, Dee!" Long Tooth yelled from the back. Mac was silent. Nick drooled in and out, head knocked back every time we hit a bump, only waking up to scratch and rub his nipples. "So who did the shit?" I yelled to the car.

"He my cousin, but fuck that clown!" said Mac.

"Your cousin?" I pulled over. "Nick, get up!"

Nick was out of it. Long Tooth said that Dog Boy got into an argument with Hurk over a hundred dollars and Hurk shot him. An awkward silence entered and then chilled the car for a few minutes.

"Yo, so y'all gonna kill Hurk?"

Mac said hell yeah because he has work and doesn't pay, he's goes to clubs just to start fights, and borrowed money from everybody in the car—saying he needed it because he's on the run, but he's always out every weekend throwing money, trying to impress girls, and he just bought a new car.

Nick rose from the dead. "I tried da tell you but shit was crazy!"

I hadn't been in the street for a few months. Running the bar was a seven-day-a-week, seven a.m. to two a.m. gig, so I really didn't know what was happening with my friends. I was busy learning how to create a schedule, hire good employees, renovate the units, and basically build my business.

"So y'all wanna kill Hurk?" I said.

"What we post to do?" Nick said.

What were they supposed to do? What was I supposed to do? My childhood best friend shot another one of my best friends and I'm in the middle. Hurk hit an all-time low; we were a family. How could you shoot your brother, someone you said you loved, over something ridiculous as money? The money changes everybody. And now I'm in a car full of my brothers ready to kill one of our brothers over money.

"Yo, I can't let y'all kill Hurk, man. This can't go down," I said.

"Well, don't be surprised if that nigga kill you!" Long Tooth replied, exiting the car.

"What's the move then?" Mac asked. "I'm fucked up and he

ain't put me on after I got locked up for his bullshit! I got my reasons for wantin' to rock that nigga, he a whole rat!"

I told Mac to relax. A part of this wasn't even about Dog Boy, it was about money. Mac was ready to kill Hurk—his real lifeblood—over money. Tyler and Troy barely called me after I stopped selling drugs. Hurk and Mac are as worthless to each other as I am to Tyler and Troy because they want money and the love fades as soon as the cash does—pure, innocent relationships gone flat over something as simple as a dollar.

"Look, Mac, I can't put you on with drugs because I don't do that anymore but I can give you five thou until you get right."

"So what I gotta do for that?"

"Just don't kill Hurk, and give me a chance to squash their beef."

"Man, I swear you the best nigga I ever met, Dee. Real life, I ain't never gonna front on you. Don't worry 'bout LT, I'll rap to him."

I pulled back over to Madeira Street and let Mac out. Nick just slept in the car for another half hour or so. Angie came out and said that Dog Boy was good but she still made him rest. We sat together on her chipped steps. I wanted to tell her that I loved her but I didn't know how—I was still learning how emotions worked from Soni—and Miss Angie's from the same slum as me.

"The neighborhood changed a lot since you left. It used to be fun round here, Dee. It felt like family. Now these young kids is crazy."

"Everybody always say that. Like every generation gets more and more crazy!"

"It's true boy! Now take me to your bar, and I want to meet your pretty girlfriend again," Angie had told me. I nodded yes. She was right; the neighborhood was different—new fiends and new drug crews. Packs of kids I never saw. Even they were new to the block or shot up really quick in the time I left. The game doesn't stop. A lot of these dudes don't know me or probably care about what I did on these streets. And they'll last a summer or two and then a new set will move in. I'm lucky enough that I was able to move on.

240 WILSON STREET

Joan picked Soni and I up on a Sunday to look at houses in Bolton Hill. A few more popped up since our last conversation. Dog Boy tagged along. I couldn't talk him out of warring with Hurk, but we still hung out every free moment I got. Joan parked on Park Avenue and told us that there were three houses we just had to see—all walking distance from one and other. The first was 240 Wilson Street.

We walked in and it felt like home.

The living and dining room was connected by endless walnut colored hard woods like a NBA regulation basketball court and making the kitchen look a mile away from the front door. The ceilings had to be like twenty feet high with low hanging double bladed fans chopping in each room. I had seen those same fans at Home Depot before—they operated by remotes and went for $400 apiece.

Soni and Dog Boy were on mute as the listing agent gave us the tour. Their jaws hung as their big eyes drank everything in sight. The agent showed us that Viking Stove Joan was raving about— saying how the burners were brass flames and boast like 20,000 BTUs across the front with multiple 15,000 BTUs and one 8,000 BTU burner across the back in addition to a bunch of stuff I never heard of. I played it cool like, "That's nice man that's really nice." The kitchen also had a matching Viking wine rack and a Viking

225

fridge that was taller than me all sitting on a collection of huge marble slabs. I imagined myself strolling through in a white Polo robe lighting a Cohiba on the stove and then pouring a half glass of some aged wine from South Africa or something like a boss.

There were three huge bedrooms on the second floor with the same quality wood floors and high ceiling fans as well. The smallest room could be my private study. I didn't really study anything but I thought I'd have to if lived in this place. The third and largest bedroom on the second floor had a midsize Jacuzzi. Dog Boy leaped in "I'ma be in here like Puff singing, I love it when you call me Big Poppa! Throw ya hands in the air, If you a true playa!"

"Actually the Puff Daddy style tub is up another level," the agent said.

We followed him up to the brilliant master suite. It was a loft style floor with an even larger Jacuzzi and bidet. I asked the agent what that other toilet was for and Dog Boy said "Don't you watch cribs? It rinse your ass after you shit for real!" Soni agreed but said, "Watch your mouth man!"

I was sold. I didn't even need to see the other houses. We looked at them but I can't remember them. 240 Wilson Street was the spot. I thought about the house every second of every day—it became the topic of 90 percent of my conversations. Every friend, customer and family member heard, "Yo the floors! Yo the kitchen! Yo the square feet!"

Joan and Lass didn't make it any easier. Together, they both kept telling me that I was preapproved for the $600k and all I had to do was pull the trigger.

Yeah it was $600k.

THE SIGNS

You think we need that house?" I asked Soni.

"No, but you really want it and I want it for you, plus I know you won't stop until you buy it! I'm not even going to front, that is the nicest place I ever been in! Straight George Jefferson status over night!"

Owning this place would be easy if I sold drugs—a few thousand a month was change. The bar wasn't really generating as much money as I thought it would. The lounge was empty and the Koreans up the street had cut rate sales on lock. They mastered the game with prices that were Walmart low—I wasn't even sure how they stayed in business. I had cash saved up and a small rental property income coming in but that wasn't nearly enough to justify that purchase.

I stalked the house for two weeks wondering how it could be mine. No one had bought it; they didn't even get an offer so I knew it was for me. I racked my brain and came up with a plan of hiring party promoters to pump up my bar so that we could generate more traffic. They can take the door money and I could jack the liquor prices. A few promoters had been reaching out to me but I never really set anything up. I called some of the most popular dudes in the city and they told me that my place was too small— unless I got rid of the poker machines.

The poker machines were clunky, dusty, and unplugged. Each

machine had the same tin label on the back that read *John Goldman (410) 555-5755*. I remembered Miss Lonnie, the previous owner, telling me that the machines didn't come with the bar, so I hit the owner up and told him to come get them.

A day or so later a Wall Street–AIG–stock–broking–looking white dude walked into the bar and peeked threw the window. I thought he was lost—a clean junkie in the early stages of addiction or a federal agent. I walked to the front window.

" 'Sup man, can I help you? "

"Why, yes you can. I work with Mr. Goldman, and I'd like to be buzzed in please."

I hit the switch and let dude in. He rubbed his hand across the glass. "All this bulletproof glass is a nice touch. I also like how it's so foggy. You can't see anything back here."

"Yeah, I'm changing that, but where is your crew? Doesn't look like you are dressed to move machines."

He pulled up a chair. "Please have a seat, Dee. Could I please borrow a moment of your time? " I pulled up a stool. He had on Gucci loafers and shiny cuff links that gleamed a little brighter than his Yacht-Master Rolex.

"So Mr. Goldman sent me here because he wants to keep your business. We are willing to offer a $5,000 loan if you keep the machines in here. You don't have to pay us out of pocket, we can take your payments directly from the proceeds of the machine. Whadoya say! I'll have a check dropped off in an hour or so."

I told him I didn't need a $5,000 loan and I was kind of offended at the way he waltzed in giving orders and rubbing glass.

"I deeply apologize, Dee, how's $7,500? "

"Why are you so eager to loan me money I'm not asking for, and what's the deal with these old machines? Do they even work? "

"Well, Dee, they do work, very well when plugged in. You see, they are digital slot machines that pay out. Your customers can come in, have a drink, and then play the slots, just like they are in Vegas! You'll be responsible for cashing them out when they hit, I'll reimburse you, and then we split everything else fifty-fifty." He spoke slowly and finished with an enthusiastic stir. I sat still for a second and thought about all of the poker machines in Baltimore. They were right in front of me my whole life and I ignored them. I knew who played them but I never knew they were lucrative. You can find one in every corner store from African-owned to Asian-owned and I guessed addiction was the reason, like everything else.

"So, why would I pay you? Why can't I just buy my own?"

"Great question, Dee. You should do business with us because we are going to give you a $10,000 loan to be paid back by the machines, fix them whenever they break and if the police raid you for paying out, which happens all of the time, we'll get you new machines within the same day. Do we have a deal?"

"So wait, you can go to jail? Forget that man, I don't need the hassle and stop talkin' that loan shit man."

He reached into his pocket and pulled out a stack of business cards. "I apologize, sir. We can sit here and call any of my clients or visit them. I will guarantee that you will never ever do a day in jail for anything related to these machines. When the cops raid, they just take the machines and the money out of your register. You may get a fine, and we'll pay that plus reimburse you for the money they take. We'll also give you $10,000, not to be paid back. Think of it as a gift from Mr. Goldman."

"A $10,000 gift? Really?"

I asked for the cards. I wanted to call some of these owners for myself. I checked out a few of his locations on the east and west side—the dude was legit. Mrs. Lonnie also gave me a call and said the guy was cool. I trusted her the most; she reminded me of an innocent grandma and knew Mr. Pete.

The dude came back through a few days later with an even better suit on. I stopped scraping crud off of the aging floor tile to buzz him in.

"Dee, I have a check for you in the amount of $10,000. Are you ready to move forward?"

"Aye, what's your name?"

"So pleasant of you to ask. I'm Ron, Ron Franklyn."

"So listen Ron, you guys checked out but 10 ain't enough."

He asked if he could have a minute to call his boss. I sat back and lit a cigar. The first pull burned my chest and made me hack until some tears spilled. Cigars were new to me, but I liked the taste and the dizzy spell they gave me—not as good as weed but legal and cool looking.

"Dee, I'll write you a check for $15,000 and we can start tomorrow. Some of your customers have been going to other locations because of the change in ownership. But once the word gets out, you are going to make a lot of money. This is a great location!"

"One thing, though," I said, "I don't take checks."

Ron came back with a contract and $15,000 in hundreds. I didn't sign the contract, but I took the money. We plugged them up and he gave me a quick tutorial on how they worked.

"Well, Dee, we are in business now!"

"I guess so."

THE BUSINESS PLAN

It took a few months to get it, but when I got it, I got it, and what I mean by got it is that I was getting it on all four levels of my store. The basement stored alcohol, wine, beer, malt liquor, and the potato-skin hooch that my second-floor tenant Mrs. Yancey made. It all lined across the back wall in Hellmann's jars next to my La-Z-Boy because that was also my chill spot where I wrapped and rolled, and puffed, and sipped.

The steps were hidden under a panel behind the bar. I'd scale down into the stock room to get away from all of the bullshit on the first floor. Opening that freezer door kept it chill in the summer and the sweaty pipes that extended out from the furnace warmed up my winters. I loved that spot; I would stay in there alone for days.

The first floor was all lounging, partying, ass-clapping, over-priced cut-rate over-the-counter shit, fried dinners, drinking, fighting, regurgitating, gambling, shit talkin', shit taking, watching the fight, starting the fight, networking, stealing, stripping, sleeping, stinking till reeking, baby showers, bridal showers, repasts, after hours, after after hours, bachelor parties, bachelorette parties, drug abuse, drug sales, and drunks pissing everywhere but the inside of our toilets.

I booked a bunch of parties and events. We rocked seven days a week—didn't matter if we had one customer or went over the zoning capacity—we rocked from six a.m. until two a.m. or three a.m. or four a.m. or whatever. We had strippers on the first Friday of every month and the popularity led to us having them every week—just because we could. It could have been a slow Wednesday or a snowy Tuesday, but everybody in that hood knew that it might be stripper night—any night could be stripper night—or dollar crabs, or buy one get one, or something. I took care of the locals and the regulars, and they took care of me.

The second floor was Mrs. Yancey's, and she held it down. She knew me from the neighborhood, and told me that she needed a spot to crib and that she got a check from the state which she would sign over to me. I knew she was a fiend but I didn't care because most people are, so I rented her the spot for $510 a month and she charged other fiends $300 a month to stay—six to be exact, so that's $1,800 a month for Mrs. Yancey minus my $510—everybody won.

Mrs. Yancey was the best tenant ever. She was dope and on dope and sold her methadone prescriptions to buy dope. She would get high at five a.m. and clean the shit out of that building—every inch, every speck, leaving my corner, my car, and my bar spotless, and it only got better when she sublet her spot. More fiends on morphine means the more clean everything is what I used to say—literally. My big homie Donnie—Mrs. Yancey's boyfriend—lived there too, and he was cool as shit with a broke-off Kangol hat. He called me his block-headed nephew. I gave him a new job every day ranging from my doorman to my DJ to the trash man to the guy who I sent to the store. Fiends like him checked for me more than their own kids because I kept money in their pockets.

The top floor was like a ho house, but not really, because I didn't house hos, I just left it open for sex—meaning that fifty-five dollars would allow you to BYOG (Bring Your Own Girl) for one hour in a room with an air mattress, a blanket, a flat-screen (TV), a variety of lotions, a can of Febreze, a mirrored ceiling, and bootleg cable. And I always—I repeat always—kept a fishbowl full of Magnums by the door. And of course the locals and regulars got to use the room for extended amounts of time at a discounted rate—because they kept me from being robbed or shot every night.

COP UP

Bo chugged back a pint glass of Jack. "I had a clothing company and it failed! A nightclub and it failed! And it's all because of these hatin'-ass niggas in this town, crabs in a barrel in Baltimore!"

Soni rolled her eyes and walked out. Baltimore's known for crabs and we normally buy them live in barrels. If you open the barrel and look in, you'll see them pulling each other down so that no crab reaches the top. Many in the Black community feel like their brothers and sisters pull them down in the same manner and use the "crabs in a barrel" as an analogy to justify their shortcomings.

I pulled him another cup. "Maybe your clothes were corny and your nightclub was wack," I said. "I'm sick of everybody in this city blaming that crabs in the barrels crap for their failures without self-reflecting! I know a bunch of people with clothing lines and clubs here getting money! If my bar fails, I gotta figure a way to make it pop!"

"No Dee, you'll see. Baltimore people are crabs and they want to see you fail! Now give my check nigga!"

"Well, Bo, you ever think that a crab's natural habitat is not a barrel? And do you know what's on the other side of that barrel? A steaming pot of death! Think about that. $14.50. The last one was on me." Bo knocked back his last drink and waddled his musky three-hundred-pound frame sideways through the front entrance. Bo and about six guys just like him became our regulars, plus our overall traffic increased a little. Enough for me to hire a few barmaids.

I noticed I'd left $2,000 in the payout box of one of the poker machines and it was gone in two days. A few people won $30 or $40 while I was around but I didn't get how and why so much money was disappearing. One of the barmaids, LaShay, said, "The same four or five people have been coming around the time you leave out. They win a lot, boss, but I swear they put it right back in the machine." I decided to do a surprise visit. A visit during the hours when they weren't expecting me to be there.

Three customers were scattered in the lounge. A balloon-shaped woman with shiny features named Pearl sat at the machine. She was in a soiled housekeeping uniform that was as brown as her skin. Her name tag dangled. "Ya got some more quarters? Get me dem quarters girl!" she said every few minutes. Her hair was finger waved and thinning around the edges—like she was one perm away from being bald.

"I'm done for the night, cash my $75 out! Des machine whipped my ass tonight!" she said to me. I told her she'd get them the next time. "Boy, I work eighty-two hours last period and about sixty of those hours went into these damn machines! I better get them back!"

I had LaShay pull her a free drink. I felt obligated to do something. At least you got a feeling with drugs; she was just aimlessly dumping money. Everyone knows that slots don't pay. After she finished her drink, she went and put the rest of her money into the machine. The payout logs said that we spent roughly $7,000 on jackpots. Ron had called me earlier that week and said he was sending out one of his collectors to settle up on Friday.

The next day I made a ton of Home Depot runs. I hate Home

Depot because the parking sucks and you always end up coming out of the opposite side of the store. Plus I'm not what you would call a traditional "Do-it-yourselfer." I don't get excited about building cabinets or hanging drywall. I'm actually a "Pay-somebody-elser," and that's exactly what I was doing. I had to fix some small issues for Mrs. Yancey. And I'm from the hood which means I didn't pay attention to pedestrian things like permits or zoning and I never heard of a licensed contractor.

We normally get the most talented junkies from around the way to rehab properties. The good thing about that is they can do the same quality of work as a professional for a fraction of the price and the down payment is normally a blast. The bad side is that they always forget something and you end up going to Home Depot ten thousand times in a day.

Nick was on the steps of the bar after my last store run. Soni had texted me earlier, saying that he's been past like two or three times already—we just kept missing each other. He wore the same dry-rotted look as the dope fiends I'd been lugging around all day.

"Brudda I need you. We 'bout to be back!" he yelled, like he hadn't seen me in years. I'd only been out of the game a few months, but that's a decade in the streets. I let the fiends into the apartment and told Nick that we could take a ride. He stunk my car up as we whipped down Lombard. I cracked every window and stuck my head out of the sunroof even though it was freezing out.

"I stink bro bro. I stink cuz I been on the block like old times. We gonna get right tho, you wanna dope?" he said aiming a fist-full of Percs at me. "These dem big ass 30's baby!"

"I don't pop Percs anymore man. And you should stop man. It's time to stop all that dumb shit. We are getting older man, lucky to be here, just chill man."

Nick shook his head and said, "Run down the projects right quick, gotta drop some money to my shorty I'm havin a li'l son."

"Congrats man! That's the news I want to hear! Tell me stuff like that man, and get off the pills, you don't want your son have a pilled-out pops!"

I paralleled on Caroline Street. Nick exited and made a right through Douglass Court. He's really having a baby, that's crazy. I think I want kids one day but only if I'm stable. I don't want to be a dad that has to figure things out—I want money and time stacked up. I want to be able to take my child on trips and expose them to something more than Baltimore and my crazy mentality. Can't have my kids knowing about selling drugs, shootouts, and the rest of the wild stuff I battled through. Nick hopped back in the car. "Yo I wanna holler at Miss Angie, and drop her a few dollars. Let's ride down the block," I said.

"So Dee. I need some money my nigga. We finna be back like I said bro, Nick and Dee, just like it was."

"Back like what?"

Nick told me that he hooked up with some dudes and was ready to build Madeira Street back up. He said some bodies had to fall but we were going to get the block back. I told him that maybe he should rock with Troy and Tyler because the block-game was dead. People don't even sell drugs in alleys anymore, it's all about cell phones.

"Naw, fuck Troy horny ass, and Tyler look like a snitch." We pulled up in front of Angie's. Some young kids struggled for loose sales. It's like it was more dealers than customers. Angie wasn't home and I really wasn't feeling the stuff that Nick was talking so I told him, "Sober up and holler at me in the a.m."

He said cool and we split. I drove back over to the bar. The machine guy Ron had called, and said that he was on his way. We arrived around the same time. First we verified the payout logs and mine matched exactly what he said—then we split the money up.

We counted up the $7,000 I spent in payouts and he gave me that. Then we split up another $15K—$7,500 for them and $7,500 for me. It blew my mind. Who knew these rusty junk boxes would be so lucrative! I felt like I was selling dope again! But in a much safer way. My first thought was why should I be splitting the money with these clowns when I could just buy my own machines, but I figured that I'd give it a few months before I cut them out.

Dude bagged his cash and slid. I tucked mine and called my lady. "Baby, we buying that house!" The phone dropped and she screamed loud enough to rupture something. I knew she wanted that house as bad as I did.

I hung up on her scream and dance routine and hopped on the horn with Joan. She set everything up. Same deal, same title spot, except I brought a cashier's check for $35K. This down payment was cheaper than the other because it was residential. My mortgage would be $4,000 a month and the machines paid that plus more.

BOLTON BUBBLE

My first year running Stadium Hideaway breezed. The money wasn't great but it was steady. Steady enough to sustain my vacuum of a mortgage. And I didn't care that the house sucked up every nickel as I watched my profits leave the register and go straight to my mortgage, second mortgage, and property tax, because I loved living in Bolton Hill.

I liked walking over those clean streets to the park on Park Avenue. Art students walked past with easels and patched jackets and backpacks, my neighbors looked happy—in the mist of all the craziness in Baltimore city, they looked happy. I even saw a woman sitting on her front playing a harp one day. It felt like I was living in a bubble—and the bubble was called high property tax.

I still had some drug money put up. Enough to not know how low my cash flow really was. My new legit stash was tucked next to my old street stash creating the illusion of me experiencing success. To celebrate, I traded my 500 in at R & H Motors and bought a hundred-thousand-dollar car—a silver CL600 with a V12 engine. That car made me lots of friends. I felt like people wanted autographs. Cops pulled me over—over and over again—and it was nothing they could do because I was cool, my papers were straight, and I wasn't in the drug game. "You should come to the happy hour at my bar, Stadium Hideaway on Lombard Street!" I'd tell them. "A lot of girls are there and our drinks are cheap enough for you to afford!"

I had the hottest car in the city and nowhere to go so I ended up going back on Madeira Street. Nick built a little crew up. The only guy who was around from my day was Fat Tay—still funky and still chasing those little girls. Dog Boy was sitting for a gun charge. He and Hurk turned the neighborhood to the Wild Wild West, shooting at each other every time they crossed paths. Mac kept his promise and kept LT from killing Hurk but Dog Boy was a different story. Nobody could control Dog Boy.

Mac and I begin to develop a close relationship. We hooped every day, doubled dated, and bought all of the same Jordans and Nike Uptempos. He was also one of my only east side friends who came to my bar every day. Mac was still in the street and I was on a mission to pull him out. I gave him money for trade school, got him a job selling cars, and even tried to find a business that we could do together, but no dice. It started feeling like the street fame was more important to Mac than the money that came with it.

We sat in the bar after the after-hours one night and I tried to teach him how life gives out rules, and it was up to us to master these rules, benefit from the ones that played in our favor and then break the ones that we could get away with.

"For example," I said, "we are street niggas. We start out in the hood that's full of junkies and dealers. The cops are racist and the teachers only show up to get paid so they don't care if we make it or not. That's the hand we start with!"

"So you saying that we ain't gonna be shit anyway?"

"No, man, I'm saying that once we acknowledge that these are our hurdles, and that the goal is for us to die or go to jail, only then can we make a plan to beat those odds. I got off the block and switched to wholesale because everybody on the block falls off. It's a failed system. I stopped selling drugs because everybody gets caught. And when I notice another obstacle, I'll switch it up again."

"You talk all that shit, Dee, cuz you ain't gotta record. I got charges, kids and some other shit you don't know about!" he said with wet red eyes, guzzling his big red plastic cup of gin and pouring another.

"Yeah, I don't know your whole life, but I know games, and this is a game. When selling drugs, my goal was to wake up, hit my quotas, duck cops, duck haters, keep my life, and stay out of jail. That was the game and I approached it just like that. That's why I'm not dead and that's why I don't have any real enemies except the dudes who didn't like me anyway."

"And what game are you playing now, Dee? What's this game?"

"This game is about hitting my quotas, ducking cops, ducking haters, keeping my life, and staying out of jail. The cops are still racist and I guess I approach it the same, except alcohol is a legal drug. Legal drugs, same bullshit."

We toasted our cold cups and laughed.

"On some real shit, Dee, you can't relate to my situation cuz you speak different. Nigga. you probably gonna be a millionaire off of some legal shit anyway and you don't even know it. You like a real-life genius nigga and you don't even know it."

I looked down at my phone and saw that LT was blowing it up—I missed like fifteen calls from him so I hit back.

Ring ring ring . . .

"Yo, Dee, you good?"

"Yeah, LT, wassup?"

"Yo, they murdered Uncle Gee, man, he got killed at the club tonight!"

REMEMBER UNCLE GEE

Bucket Head spotted me sitting by myself on east Fayette Street by the courtyard. He threw his hazards on and jumped out the driver's side.

"Ain't you Gee, young boy?" he asked as he staggered over. He walked and sounded like a war vet with stiff joints. He stood about five-foot-nothing with a face made of eyes and patchy stubble.

"Yeah, Bucket, I remember you!" I said, reaching for a handshake, but he pulled me in deep for a hug—an uncomfortable one, the hugs where two people lock, exchange smells and rock back and forth and back and forth.

"You just got out?" I said.

"Five minutes ago! How you know?" Ignoring the fact he smelled like a cellblock, we both looked down at the huge DOC logo on his shirt and laughed.

"This my last time going in! I'm staying home this time, but boy, your uncle Gee sure did make jail fun back in the day! I miss him!"

Gee's big face eclipsed the clouds as Bucket spoke, and I swear he saw it too because he let out a huge chuckle and said, "I remember when Gee had the jail on lock! We were co-dees on a shooting and sat for two years. Gee was running the jail two weeks into our bid. He had gangstas rolling his socks and folding his clothes into

242

triangles, making him jelly sandwiches, and peeling the edges off of the bread—he'll beat your ass if you don't take them edges off. COs stuck heroin balloons up their asses and smuggled them in for Gee and he sold it all. He had me selling it and I even made enough to pay for my daughter's everything, from jail! We were getting money. Gee made five thousand dollars a week in jail! No, Gee made ten thousand, actually Gee made ten thousand every time he tried to make money even if he didn't really try. I'm telling you boy, the warden had to really, really rely on your uncle to end prison riots. Gee had that jail on lock!"

I remember when he came home from that stretch back when I was eleven. He told us that he owned that jail and showed us the cash. He gave a fist full to me and bought me a new PW50 for my birthday. That was my first dirt bike, my baby. I washed it every day, even in the winter, until my hands ashed and bled.

Gee taught me how to wheelie and how to stop traffic and how to fuck traffic up and how to never get caught. He rode a big CR250. I was too small to ride it, but he let me sit on it and told me I could be the best one day, even better than him if I tried.

Bucket Head rambled on like, "One real thing about your uncle is that he never forgot about the dudes on lockdown. Yo! After Gee came home he always sent us pictures over the jail of him wheeling bikes past a zillion people in awe. Wish I was home, man, wish I could've saw that, I would've rode too. I heard he got drunk one time and rode the bike butt naked with a mink on and some gators and some Chanel frames with the lenses poked out in the middle of the summer during a heat wave. They say he fell off and scarred his belly. I heard he popped up, did the running man and then pissed on a cop in a cop car!"

We laughed. I remembered that for sure, I told him I was right there; we rode forty bikes deep every day that summer. That's when I honed my skills. I fell more times than him as a sober kid. He pissed on the cop car, but the cop wasn't in there. He pissed on everything that summer—his girlfriends, cop cars, park benches, the door at Hecht Company, the chip section at Unz Market, floral arrangements, nodding fiends...

Bucket said, "I remember he pissed a lot. He had a big heart and a little bladder or something like that. But he definitely violated parole for pissing on that cop. I remember. We were rotting in Jessup where they tried to feed us bags of white rice mixed with white roaches—weebles is what we called them. Fucking weebles."

"It wasn't a cop car though, Bucket," I said. I was there, I remember. It was for assaulting a DJ at this club called The Paradise Lounge. I was fifteen, so I paid a hundred dollars to get in. Every night was ladies night. Gee wanted to hear some DMX, actually we all did. So Gee yelled, "Yo, cut some X on!" to the DJ. The DJ waved in disapproval. He was playing R. Kelly or something like that, I didn't care—I was young and ass watching. Gee said, "Yo, cut some DMX on, where ma dawgs at! Come on!" The DJ pointed to his tag that read "DJ" and waved Gee off again.

Gee laughed, climbed to the top of the booth, pistol-slapped the DJ, ripped his DJ tag off and threw him into the crowd. Then Gee pumped DMX at the highest level; the club shook and cracked the Richter scale as he yelled, "DJ Gee in the house! Where my dawgs at!" Everyone barked just like DMX. Gee transformed the club into a kennel. The DJ slipped out the front door with a blood-leaking dome. He and the cops were out front waiting for DJ Uncle Gee when the club closed.

"You right, shorty," said Bucket "I remember now because he

sat for minute and his li'l man Bip was murdered. He was fucked up over that. I remember he stomped on a dude until his chest caved in; it took seven COs to pull him off of that kid. He did his bid in the hole and had that accident right after he came home."

I told him that I'll never forget that because Bip was my brother. Bucket shouted, "RIP Bip! But nothing could stop Gee. I remember he started to tell a white man, black man, Chinese man joke and stopped in the middle to shoot somebody!"

I remembered that too because he dragged the body off into the alley, came back out and finished the joke. And that's Gee.

Extra flashy and would shoot you in a second always yelling, "Yay Down the Hill! Yay Down the Hill!" Even tatted it on his chest. Even made into a song and sang it while waving his arms like a victory flag—stomping a kid down in Club Choices.

He stomped a coma into that kid's future.

I dipped into my pocket and pulled out a jay. It was stuffed with buds spilling from both ends.

"If you pass that, I'm blow it with you," said Bucket. I sparked, puffed twice, and passed.

"Can't believe one shot took your uncle, man."

I told him that Gee was murdered at Strawberry's 5000. They say he threw money at some girls hanging by the bar—literally. They weren't strippers; they were working women, probably underpaid assistant nurses or something. Everyone watched him, like they always did. Gee took his shirt off and ran around the club with two Cristal bottles. He liked to walk around drinking them like they were bottled waters. They say he bumped bouncers who were too scared to react and knocked around gangsters who knew he was an ass when drunk. No one stopped him because no one could, that was Gee being Gee. Twenty or more of his close friends and family members around and no one stopped him.

Gee knocked a kid named Chip down. Chip said, "Damn, Gee! Chill the fuck out!" They say Chip had no real beef but you couldn't just tell Gee to chill the fuck out.

Right, right, and a strong overhand right to Chip's nose. Heard he deflated like a broken air mattress. Stomps came next, heavy Timberland boots rained on Chip's body.

The police rushed in and broke everything up.

They say it was over. Chip was all bloody and could barely walk to his truck, Gee called him, knife in hand: "Come here, bitch!" Chip spun around and gave Gee one chest shot in front of the cops. The ambulance stayed away just long enough for Gee to die.

"We had a little memorial for him over the jail. RIP Gee," said Bucket, shaking his head in despair.

"Welcome home, Bucket," I replied, giving him another dap.

I'M IN THE NBA

Our Bose speaker box linked up with Kanye West and yelled, "I graduated and you can live through anything if Magic made it!" I cranked it on the highest level and sat it next to Soni's ear.

"Stopppppppppp! I'm asleep! Get away from me!" she yelled, swinging at me with a right and then a left hook.

I cut the music off, snatched the half blunt off of my dresser and went downstairs to pour a big cup of vodka and ice. Soni could sleep late all she wanted, I was going to celebrate for her. She had passed her last final and was graduating from Johns Hopkins University. The first college graduate that I had ever met was sleeping upstairs in my bed. I was inspired by her. The Gee news and his funeral had me in the dumps but her excellence shot my spirits right back up as her accomplishment and insight normally do. Her graduating was a landmark in her life and mine, so we had to celebrate this the right way.

Mac and I were in a basketball league and we had a game later that day. I opened the bar, let my workers in, and scooped him from over North East Market. He hopped in my car with a smile that connected both of his ears. "Yo, I'm gonna do a big coke deal and then I'm out the game! Man, I got a sick plug, he gonna bless me and I'ma be done with this street shit!"

"You talking that coke deal with Nick? That dumb stuff he

talking about?" I asked because he had been sending word to me about some made-up *Scarface* deal for two hundred bricks of cocaine that would set us for life. I felt bad because I thought he'd finally lost his mind.

"Hell no, I ain't talkin' no deal with his fat junkie ass! Me and LT got sumthin' poppin'! We gonna plug Dog Boy when he come home too! You want in?"

"I'm out! For the billionth time, but I could use the money because I'm about to go cop a whip!"

Mac cut the music off. "Nigga, what's wrong with this Benz!"

I told him that my Benz was great but it wasn't about me. Today was about Soni. She once told me that those hardtop-convertible Lexus SC430's were cute, so I wanted to surprise her with one for a graduation present. I saw a pretty black one in the paper. Mac and I drove up to Prestige Motors out in the county and I bought it—ten thousand down and dude gave me the key. The car was a year old, slightly used but the inside smelled like new sneakers, she's going to love this.

Mac followed me in my ride back to my place. We parked my car a block away so Soni wouldn't know I was around. She texted me an apology for being cranky, and I left her a vague response. Figured I'd make her sweat a little bit.

Mac and I went to our game. He put on a show, scoring forty out of the sixty points our team had put up. He was truly the best player in the gym.

"Great game, Mac!" echoed as we left.

We made it to Michaels arts and crafts just in time for me to buy a ribbon big enough to wrap the car with.

"Man, you just like an NBA dude!" he said as I dropped him off on his block. "I'm rocking like this after my last deal!"

"Get your money man," I said.

We dapped each other and I pulled off.

Mac was right. I was like an NBA dude. I had the woman, the cars, the huge crib, the fans, the YSL, the Gucci, the trips, the love, and I'm on my way home to my hot tub after playing ball. I had everything I wanted, but I still felt fucked up. My cash flow was low and was going to be really low with this new car note, but that wasn't the main issue, because I was depressed with my friends and the decisions they were making. I couldn't do anything to save any of them—they are all going to end up in jail or like Gee.

I took the long way home and thought about the bar business. What's the difference between owning my liquor store and selling dope? I'm still preying on addictions. The slot machine huggers and the bottle huggers are the same as the people I used to get heroin and crack to.

I pulled over by a cut-rate, bought a fifth of Absolut and leaned on the Lexus. Two swigs in and I realized that I wasn't shit. My bar isn't shit, these cars ain't shit, and I'm just a ugly part of the problem. I'm a failure like I always was. Telling people to not sell drugs while I'm technically a drug dealer sounded more and more stupid. Especially since I couldn't provide an alternative—because really, what else could they do? What else could I do? I thought I'd probably die in my bar selling yak like I should've died when I was selling dope.

I drove my drunk ass home. Soni's mother's car was out front. I jammed like eight pieces of gum into my mouth so they wouldn't smell the liquor before calling her cell.

Ring ring ring...

"I've been calling you all day! Where are you at?"

"Shut up and come out front," I said.

She opened the door. "Whose car is that?"

"Yours!" I said. Her big eyes got bigger and bigger as she ran down to hug me. Her mom did the same. I made them take a test-drive without me and went into my house with my marble floors and my professional chef appliances that I never cook on.

What the fuck does it all mean?

Our dining room had a mirror that came from Pier 1—another $450 price tag. I looked in it and wondered what I would be without all of this shit. I didn't know because having things has always been a part of my identity. That smile on Soni's face was semi-purchased, and she wasn't even into material things when we met.

Money issues affected all of my relationships, from Troy to Tyler to Nick to Hurk, and what if the same thing happened to Soni and me? I'd like to think that it couldn't but who knows. Guess I'll have to wait to see what happens when the money runs out.

I DON'T WANNA BE IN THE
NBA ANYMORE

Mac made his big deal and ran up into the bar bragging about the cash. Said he was going to make a few more runs.

"What happened to chilling out?" I asked.

"Chill? Chill? Chill don't pay the bills!" he sang, peeling through a bushel of hundreds and fifties. At that point I knew I had to separate myself from him too. No more basketball leagues, double dates, or hanging out in general. It didn't really bother him. He was like anyone else. He had money and friends—new drug friends that he had made through business.

They started hanging on Rutland Avenue; I caught the lot of them sitting out one day in front of my friend Nard's house. A known collection of snitches, murderers, kids, and fake gangstas with Mac and LT in the middle. I rode by without stopping, I didn't even hit the horn. Every once in a while Mac would call to borrow my car or trade cars but I didn't. Those dudes were hotter than hell in July and staying away made me feel safe—but not complete.

"Why you look so sad?" Soni asked me one day. I was in our living room, listening to Marvin Gaye, filling a shot glass to the tip with Absolut.

"I'm good," I responded.

"I know you, Dee, I know when something is wrong with you! Tell me!"

"It's the bar," I said. "I'm tired of it."

"Oh my God! I hate that bar! It depresses me sooooo much and I knew you were sad, Dee, you need to know that you can open up to me about anything!" Big sloppy tears drenched her face and neck. I wrapped my arms around her tiny frame.

"The other day I watched Pearl put her whole check in the machine. She was crying because she was flat broke. I stopped her as she left out and gave her two hundred dollars, like, 'Just pay me when you get some money,' and then I ran to the back to grab a call. When I came back out, she had put the two hundred dollars in the machine and was broke again."

"Damn, baby, that's not your fault."

"I know it's not my fault, Soni, but I definitely ain't helping, especially not by running this addiction hub."

"Dee, you are so much more than these liquor and drug and gambling businesses. You are intelligent, charismatic, and strong. People like you can be whatever they want. Get rid of the bar!"

"I'm trying to figure something out, baby. This is all new to me. But we gotta do it right, strategically you know, because what will I do for money?"

"Fuck money, Dee! I'm a college graduate, Yo! I can get a job and take care of us! Sell this place and we'll travel the world! Sell that other house too! Happiness is more important than a bunch of material crap; I've been telling you that since I met you!"

"And what about your car?"

"Oh, I'm keeping that Lex!"

We laughed. I squeezed her again. Soni pulled away to kiss me and I wiped her remaining tears—her eyes smiled. She sighed. Her face pressed my chest as she mumbled the words, "Money doesn't matter, money doesn't matter, I just want you."

I exhaled.

It took twenty-three years for me to figure out that money and love are two different things. Until that point, my whole life had been centered around what I had, what I could do for others, or what I could make. My friends and family felt like me—we all share the same bullshit-money-equals-love mentality cocktailed with the false culture that drugs or quick money is an easy answer for everything. We are all equally flawed. Soni separated those worlds for me.

The next day I put the bar on the market just to see what was out there. I had paid $150K and listed it for $265K because the neighborhood was in the middle of being gentrified by the University of Maryland. I knew the presence of white people jogging through hoods easily justified my hundred-plus-K spike because we didn't advertise in the newspaper, hang up signs, or anything, and the listing blew up as soon as it hit the net. So many people wanted to see it.

The top prospect was a middle-aged, light-skinned dude from D.C. named Ken Simpson. He was a stereotypical business type with his corny Bluetooth earpiece, brown church shoes, and a matching clipboard.

"Will you be making any future Baltimore acquisitions, Dee?" he said as he sipped his Bud Light at the bar on a Thursday night. He came down a few consecutive Thursday nights to monitor our customer flow. Mac popped in the lobby on the night of his last visit. He was wearing a black hoodie, black Levi's, a black trench coat, and dark shades even though it was pitch black outside.

"Long time no see! Hey Mr. Ken, this is Mac, he is one of my childhood friends!" I said, as Ken extended his hand.

"Man, fuck this nigga, Dee, we need to talk!" screamed Mac. He removed the shades; beads of sweat made his forehead look like Braille.

"Excuse me, young man?" replied Ken, standing up.

"Yo, chill!" I yelled at Mac. "Man, this my people, man!"

"I'm sorry, sir, something bad happened. Dee, we need to talk!"

I walked him out front. He paced back and forth, rubbing his palms. "Yo, let's get in the car!" he said. We hopped in and slammed both doors.

"They on to us, Dee! The feds! Man, they did a sweep last night and picked up eight niggas!"

"Us? Fuck you mean, us?"

"Sorry, man, I'm just going crazy. Didn't mean to say you. But I know they comin', man, feds is in town!"

"Relax, bro," I said, pulling out of the parking spot. "How you know they want you?"

"Man, they kicked in my mother's house last night and I don't even know why they lookin' for me cuz I only got a thousand dollars, I ain't no kingpin! Plus they snatched LT and Block up too!"

I turned the radio off and we rode around for about fifteen minutes in silence. The loudest fifteen minutes of my life—every horrible thought crossed my mind, from me to Soni, to everybody being locked up. I pulled up in front of the bar.

"If the feds is on you, why you come to me?"

"Just to give you a heads-up, bro. I love you, man. I'll see you on the other side."

A week later they caught Mac in Safeway with his girlfriend and daughter. He called me saying that there were about thirty people on the indictment. They had him as a major wholesaler and he was broke. He said they asked who I was, but he told them I had a legit job. That sounded great, but I was still worried.

One thing I know about the streets is you never know who is going to tell. The softest guy will stand tall and the biggest gangsta will snitch you like, "I'm sorry, man, my mother made me do it!" Nobody can make you tell and you never know, so I was extra cautious.

I didn't want to be in the NBA anymore. The fear of losing my freedom made everything I did seem extremely stupid. I mean warring with local cops was one thing—but the United States. Mac was facing the United States of America. He had no win.

I sold the bar to Ken and walked away with around $70,000 after taxes. There was no way that I could sustain that mortgage and those car payments with no income, so I ran toward my biggest fear.

I let everything go—two repos because no one wanted to buy the cars and a big-ass foreclosure because we couldn't sell the house—the house with the mortgage that ate up most of my $70K. Soni and I took an apartment on Caroline Street, not too far from where I grew up.

NICK

I read about the case in the paper—98 percent of it was bullshit. They were connecting murders that didn't have anything to do with each other and calling it gang related or organized crime all in an effort to make their case look better. There was no organization and no gangs, just childhood friends who shared customers and liked to hang out. The first paragraph of the article had at least three different sets of dudes from three different neighborhoods that they identified as a single gang.

I wouldn't be surprised if Johns Hopkins Hospital had something to do with it because they conveniently swooped in and sucked up the neighborhood after the indictment. They even moved Miss Angie to the suburbs. She loved the idea of living in the county until she realized that she would no longer be able to walk to her favorite cleaners, the supermarket, and her church.

I saw Nick near where we used to hang, or what was left of it. His husky frame dissolved and sagged. He could no longer fill his big 4X clothes. I sat in the car for a second and watched him laugh and joke with children half his age—his new peers.

"Nick, wassup!"

He pulled a pistol from his waist and pointed it. "Fuck you want to be up, nigga?"

"Man, your old dirty ass ain't shooting shit!" one of the kids yelled.

"It's me, Dee!"

"You almost caught a hot one!" he said, approaching my car, and waving off the laughing kids. "Where the six at?"

I hopped out and told him that I had to move the six and the house because I didn't have an income. "I'm happy to have this Honda!"

"Let's go to ya bar, Dee! Get a nigga fucked up."

"That's gone too!"

We walked to the basketball court and watched wiry teens battle it out in a game of two on two.

"Yo, you wanna get next?" I asked.

"Naw, I can't breathe right," he said. "But I do gotta big play for us, man, glad you slid by, boy!"

Nick asked me to put $60K of my own money with $100K of his and another guy's cash into this big deal that could get us ten bricks of cocaine. I couldn't afford it, and I didn't want to do it. Enough was enough, and I knew that he didn't have that type of money anyway. If he did, he probably would've been shooting up, and he probably wouldn't stink, and I probably wouldn't be able to see his toe through his Nike.

"I don't sell drugs, man, you heard what just happened to Mac and them?"

He pushed away from the gate and reached out for a handshake. I slapped his palm—he squeezed mine and pulled me in closer. "Well, nigga, I suggest you stay away from here, cuz if you wasn't my nigga, I'll take what you have and kill you!"

I pushed him off me. "Do what you gotta do!"

He pulled out the gun, pointed it at me and said, "Bow!" and then walked down the block. That was the last time I saw Nick. It felt like that Nas song that goes "A thug changes and love changes and best friends become strangers."

I heard Nick started raising his money through an old-school approach. He hit every block from east to west, shaking down dealers, jamming his gun down throats, and emptying the pockets of anyone selling anything. I heard he even hung a kid out of a window for three hundred dollars—any and every thing to get the money he was looking for.

We have a saying in east Baltimore that goes "Stick-up kids don't last long" and it's right. Some guys from one of the many crews Nick robbed caught up with him and blew his brains out on Ashland Avenue, steps away from where we used to hustle.

A huge part of my life was gone, but strangely, I found a piece of happiness in Nick's death. Nick wasn't Nick anymore and it was hard for me to see any change. I'm sure he could've left the streets and done something else but he never wanted to or never tried.

F.E.D.S. or *Don Diva* magazine were the only books I'd ever see him touch. He indulged on every level of the streets from fucking crackheads raw to wild shootouts, and the rush was a high like the drugs he stuffed in his body. His delayed reactions when someone asked him a question were sad. Listening to people call my friend a joke or a junkie-bitch was sad and worse than everything—seeing his short obituary was sad.

One paragraph that begins with being born at Johns Hopkins, elevates to being educated in the Baltimore City Public School System, and ends with being called home to Christ. The same tired paragraph I saw over and over again for most of my life, one of my biggest fears—not dying, but dying with the same story as everyone else.

At least he didn't have to hurt any more.

REBIRTH

I went from a $600,000 Bolton Hill brownstone to a shit apartment back in the hood. Soni got a job as a special ed teacher and I enrolled in college. This time, I attended the University of Baltimore, which is a semi-mixed school. UB ended up being a better fit for me than Loyola. It wasn't *A Different World*, but they had a few black professors. The white students at UB knew nothing about the Baltimore I'm from, but it was a mix of working people who wanted to better themselves through education, and I connected with them because of all the game I learned from Tyler.

I started out with a writing class—WRIT 100, where we had to read a book called *Fire in a Canebrake*. It was about the last mass lynching in America, which shocked me because it happened in the 1940s, which wasn't even that long ago. After completing the reading we were responsible for writing reflections on the chapter. The process of developing my own opinions on a historical event that was relevant changed me. I felt smarter three weeks into the class. The critical side of my mind grew hungry and was begging to be fed.

For the first time in my life I realized how important reading really was. I harassed the professor for more titles after class. She introduced me to writers like Langston Hughes who ended up being my favorite poet and thinkers like Michael Eric Dyson, who wrote a book about 2Pac—2Pac! I didn't even know you could write a book about 2Pac! But Sister Souljah's *The Coldest Winter Ever* was the book that hooked me on reading. I read it in a day and then read it again. The story hit really close to home, giving me perspectives of drug culture I never thought about while being deep in it. I needed more.

After reading everything Souljah wrote, I started devouring novels, articles, and everything else. You couldn't find me without a book. My mind opened all the way up and I filled it with more information and new ideas. I gained a better understanding of music and culture in general. Nas's stories made more sense, Jay Z complex rhymes became more clear and for the first time in my life, I felt like I was making decisions based on my own thoughts. Critical thinking became my obtainable super power. As a result I began to question everything—why did the government dismantle the Black Panthers but allow the KKK to function? The Black Panthers built while the Klan destroyed. Why does America praise Joe Kennedy and demonize Big Meech? They both made fortunes selling illegal drugs. The government still makes a fortune off of selling drugs. Why were the dudes involved in the Rodney King uprise called rioters but the people responsible for the Boston Tea party got to be revolutionaries? They both looted and destroyed for freedom. Why? I continued to absorb, question, and then question my questions.

I understood why my friends and I hated reading growing up. As a kid, I was given books about slaves who followed kids that painted fences by Mark Twain—not to take away from those books, but they didn't speak to us. We spent summers ducking bullets, and riding dirt bikes, so the events that Twain spoke about felt flat to us.

Bip read and he was different—he was thinker. He analyzed things and that's what reading has allowed me to do. Now I know why he cared about it so much. Way back, I spit a Douglass quote to my bro that went, "Once you learn to read, you will be forever free." I didn't really get it back then, but it is so clear now. Reading has freed me. I'm at home now.

A few books, along with my new passion for reading, helped all of my perspectives evolve and sent me on the path to purpose and an understanding of the power of education. I wanted to be able to do the same for other students, so I decided to become a teacher.

As a teacher I thought I could use my story as a way to get other kids like me—Dog Boy, Mac, Nick, and Hurk—to read. Education was working for me so I knew I could use it as tool to help somebody else, plus I could give back to the neighborhoods that my friends and I tore apart. All these college dudes rap about making it out the hood, but that's not me. Running away from issues don't solve them. Staying in East Baltimore as a teacher after I graduate could make a huge difference.

I shared my plan with some of the corny people I went to school with and they said, "Teachers don't make money!" I ignored them, because I made tons of money in the streets and happiness didn't come with it. But developing a better understanding of who I am and where I came from meant the world to me and would make my brother proud.

And making my brother proud was all I wanted to do anyway.

ACKNOWLEDGMENTS

This book is dedicated to you.

Reading Group Guide

THE

COOK UP

Reading Group Guide

THE COOK UP

1. If you were in D's position and you opened that safe, what do you think you would have done?

2. At what point does *The Cook Up* read more like a novel than a memoir? How is D's story a hero's journey?

3. How would you characterize D's choice to start cooking crack cocaine? Was it an act of veneration to try to be just like his big brother? Or by defying Bip's wish for his brother to attend college, was D's becoming a drug dealer an assertion of his independence? Bip always hoped for more for D. Who in your life does that for you?

4. D begins *The Cook Up* with a college acceptance and ends it with a college attendance, but he lived a thousand lives in between. Consider the ways D's values changed during his years away from higher education in terms of maturity, responsibility, and materialism. What if he had remained at Loyola

University and never started dealing? What did he gain from dropping out of college?

5. Discuss the ways in which the realities of running a drug ring differed from your expectations of it. Were there any stereotypes you may have had that *The Cook Up* forced you to confront? If so, what were they?

6. D refers to himself as a "serial escapist." Does this strike you as an apt characterization? What exactly is D escaping from, and does he ever succeed in outrunning it?

7. D refers to women like Miss Angie as "the most powerful people in the black community," in that she provides consistent support in a neighborhood of volatile change. In what ways does this definition upset the conventional understanding of power? By these standards, who is the most powerful person in your own life?

8. Why do you think D included Hope in his memoir? As a symbol? A warning? A turning point? Who was she to him? In their final interaction at the 7-Eleven, D and Hope fail to recognize each other. Put yourself in D's shoes: Would you have acted differently?

9. D and his friends worshiped Jay Z; they even called their product "Rockafella" to pay homage to the rapper's record label. What do you think it is about the musician that made Jay Z so iconic to this group? Who was that figure in your own life, growing up?

10. D says that as a child, he was given books such as *The Adventures of Huckleberry Finn* that he and his friends couldn't relate to. It wasn't until he discovered Laura Wexler's *Fire in a Canebrake* and Sista Souljah's *The Coldest Winter Ever* in college that D finally enjoyed reading. What books do you think should be taught in schools? Is there such a thing as a universally relatable book?

11. Discuss D's assertion that reading is the avenue to freedom, to understanding others and ourselves. When does reading make us feel closer to worlds other than our own, and when does it make us more aware of our individuality? Is one result more freeing than another? What freedoms has *The Cook Up* provided you?

ABOUT THE AUTHOR

D. Watkins is an editor at large for Salon. His work has been published in the *New York Times*, *The Guardian*, *Rolling Stone*, and other publications. He holds a master's in Education from Johns Hopkins University and an MFA in Creative Writing from the University of Baltimore. He is a college professor at the University of Baltimore and founder of the BMORE Writers Project, and has also been the recipient of numerous awards including Ford's Men of Courage and a BME fellowship. He has lectured at countless universities, and events, and programs around the country.

Watkins has been featured as a guest and commentator on NBC's *Meet the Press*, CNN's *The Erin Burnett Show*, MSNBC's *Melissa Harris-Perry Show*, *Democracy Now*, and NPR's *Monday Morning*, among other shows.

Watkins is from and lives in East Baltimore. He is the author of the *New York Times* bestseller *The Beast Side: Living (and Dying) While Black in America*.